BUSINESS
LAW

before the

'lo4

il

Crucial Study Guides for Business Degree Courses

Titles in the series

Financial Accounting	ISBN 1 903337 00 3	Price £9.99
Business Information Systems	ISBN 1 903337 01 1	Price £9.99
Microeconomics	ISBN 1 903337 02 X	Price £9.99
Business Law	ISBN 1 903337 03 8	Price £9.99
Organisational Behaviour	ISBN 1 903337 04 6	Price £9.99
Quantitative Methods	ISBN 1 903337 05 4	Price £9.99

To order, please contact our distributors:

Plymbridge Distributors, Estover Road, Plymouth, PL6 7PY
Tel: 01752 202301. Fax 01752 202333. Email: orders@plymbridge.com
www.plymbridge.com

BUSINESS LAW

Susan Heenan and Karen Moore

First published in 2002 by Crucial, a division of Learning Matters Ltd.

British Library cataloguing in Publication data
A CIP record for this book is available from the British Library.

ISBN 1 903337 03 8

Crucial
58 Wonford Road
Exeter EX2 4LQ
Tel: 01392 215560
Email: info@crucial.uk.com
www.crucial.uk.com

Cover design by Topics – The Creative Partnership
Project Management by Deer Park Productions
Typeset by Anneset, Weston-super-Mare, Somerset
Printed and bound in Great Britain by Bell & Bain Ltd, Glasgow

Contents

STUDYING LAW AS PART OF A BUSINESS DEGREE

Summary

This book is primarily intended to be a study guide for those who are studying law as part of a business degree and who may not have studied law before. It is not intended to be a substitute for attending lectures and tutorials. It covers topics which are taught on most business law courses and attempts to give a simplified explanation of those topics. It is designed to help you pick up and remember the essential points without going into depth. You will be given the opportunity to test yourself on what you have learnt in each chapter. The final chapter gives some idea of the type of questions that you may expect in an examination. Multiple choice questions (MCQ's) are becoming very popular in business degree examinations. You will be given a question with a number of alternative answers and you will be asked to choose the correct answer. You may think this will be easy but in practice you will need a broad knowledge of the whole module to do well. In addition to MCQ's you may have to answer two or more problem or essay questions.

You have obviously been successful in your studies to date but you may find studying for a degree very different from how you have studied for A levels, BTEC's or GNVQ's. This chapter explains how you can study effectively at degree level. It explains:

- how to get the most out of lectures and tutorials;

- other methods of learning that may be useful to you;

- how to prepare for assignments and examinations.

It is also important to remember the basics of studying for any subject.

Managing your time

You will probably be studying a number of subjects and you will have to allocate your time between these subjects. Do not make unrealistic targets that you cannot keep but make sure you spend as much time as you can on each subject. Make sure you use your time effectively. Do not study when you are tired. Find somewhere where you will not be interrupted. If you cannot study quietly where you live then go to the university library which will usually have a quiet study area. Take regular breaks.

Crucial tip	You may find if you check your course details that it will tell you how many hours you should spend on preparation for tutorials or assignments.

Follow instructions

You should find that you have a department notice board. Find out where your notice board is and check it daily. Follow instructions given in course and module books. Find out when and where lectures and tutorials take place. Take along what is required, such as textbooks and question sheets. When you are given questions to answer for tutorials and for assignments, make sure you have followed the instructions. If you don't understand them, ask the lecturer.

Crucial tip	Don't be tempted to buy a book at a reduced price from one of last year's students. The textbook may have changed from last year. Even if it hasn't, there may be a later version. Law textbooks become out of date very quickly as the law changes. Make sure your lecturer has confirmed which textbook and which version you must buy before you buy it.
	If you don't find the recommended textbook easy to understand there are many other textbooks which you may refer to. Check out your university library and browse through some business law books to see which book you feel you understand best.

Section 1 — How to get the most out of lectures and tutorials

Lectures usually take place in a lecture theatre with a large number of students present. Lectures aren't usually a suitable place to ask lots of questions of your lecturer as they are mainly designed to deliver information about key topics you have to cover. Tutorials (or seminars) will be small group sessions where you will be asked to prepare work in advance for discussion. It will usually be on a topic that has been covered in the lecture and you will have the opportunity to ask questions of your tutor on issues under discussion.

In the lecture you will be expected to make notes on what the lecturer has told you. You don't need to write down word for word what he or she says. Be selective. You will usually be told what are the most important points. After the lecture you should read through your lecture notes. If they don't make sense then you should read through your textbook to get a further explanation. If you still don't understand your notes then speak to another student or ask the lecturer when you have your tutorial. Don't just put your notes away hoping that you will understand them when it comes to examination time. This rarely happens.

The better student will supplement lecture notes with what he or she has read in the textbook. An examiner will be impressed to read something in an exam paper that he or she has not told you. (Of course it must be relevant!)

Use time in tutorials to gain further understanding of what you have been taught in your lectures. Make sure you prepare as much as possible in advance. Do not waste the group's time by asking the lecturer to go through what you could have read yourself. If you have prepared you will find the tutorial a much more enjoyable experience and you are more likely to remember the topic when it comes to examination time. Don't go to tutorials with blank sheets of paper not having read the work.

Crucial tip	Always attend lectures and tutorials. In our experience it is the student with poor attendance who is most likely to fail the course.
	If you are unable to attend because of illness make sure you get a copy of any handouts and speak to your lecturer or another student about what was covered.

Crucial tip	If you don't understand something then don't be afraid to ask. Most people feel extremely embarrassed about doing this in a lecture or tutorial because they think that they are the only one who doesn't understand. The chances are that there are a number of students in the same position.
	You may feel more comfortable asking questions in tutorials when there are fewer students present.

Section 2 — Other methods of learning that may be useful to you

You may have a session in the law library as a part of your module. This is extremely useful and will help you with your research for assignments and tutorials. If you don't, or even if you do, go and speak to the law subject librarian. He or she is usually extremely approachable and will be prepared to give you information about the best ways of using the library for your study. The librarian may be able to give you handouts on how to use the library and on the most useful websites for your subject.

There may be other law books that you will find useful for assignments. There may also be articles in magazines which may be more up-to-date than your textbook. The law librarian will also be able to show you what a law report looks like and how you can search for one.

Many students find that studying in groups is very beneficial to them. If you are able to get together with a number of people on your course you can share your ideas and fears. You could arrange to meet on a weekly basis.

> **Crucial tip**
>
> Try to avoid having students in your study group who aren't prepared to contribute and share the workload. Just because someone is a friend doesn't mean they will make a good study group member.

Section 3 — How to prepare for assignments and examinations

You will usually have at least one assignment during the year. Make sure you have a copy of the question and make sure you know where and when it has to be handed in. You may find this information in your course or module handbook. If you hand it in late, without good reason, you may score zero and you will have to do another piece of work. Your assignment may be an essay question, a problem question or you may have to give a presentation.

When you are writing an essay, it is important that you understand the question. Make sure you have the most up-to-date information. This may involve research in the library and on the Internet. Problem questions are very common for law assignments and for examination questions. You will be given a scenario and asked to advise one or both of the parties. To answer a problem question you should identify the relevant area of law, describe the law and then you must apply the law to the facts that you have been given in the question.

> **Crucial tip**
>
> Follow instructions. If you are asked to advise Fred, then give advice which is relevant to him. Do not write everything you know about the topic. Do not answer a question that has not been set.

If you are given a word limit then stick to it. You may be penalised for exceeding the word limit.

If you have to make a presentation, then preparation is the key. You may be given a set time for the presentation in which case it is important that you stick to that time. If you overrun then you will be asked to stop. Time yourself in advance. Make sure that your presentation is well structured. To make it more professional you may use overheads or you may use a computer package to produce slides.

Every student dreads examinations but if you have worked steadily throughout the year they should not present too much of a problem. In our experience the students who have problems are the ones who leave everything until the last minute. Students who have attended and prepared work for tutorials usually find examination preparation easier because they are used to analysing questions and preparing answers.

Before the examination

- Make sure that you have a complete set of notes.
- Attend revision sessions organised by your lecturers.
- Organise a revision timetable.
- Go through past papers. Try to answer the questions without notes and within a set time.
- Make sure you have checked the date and timing of the examination.
- Make sure you know the location of the examination room.
- Give yourself plenty of time to get to the examination.

- Avoid students who look flustered and who want to keep going over things two minutes before the examination. They will confuse you.
- Make sure you have at least two pens with you.

During the examination

- Read the examination instructions carefully. Don't answer more questions than you need to or answer too many from specific sections.
- Read the questions carefully and make sure you understand them.
- Make brief notes of relevant points you wish to refer to in the questions then you won't forget to include them when writing your answers.
- Answer your best question first.
- Try to time yourself so that you allocate an equal amount of time to each question.
- Write as clearly as you can and give yourself the best chance of obtaining extra marks.
- Don't worry if you can't remember case names or dates precisely. If you think the facts or outcome of a specific case are relevant to the question then simply state 'in a decided case'. This will show that you know there is case support for what you are saying.

Crucial tip	Don't answer questions which aren't on the examination paper. Just because you have revised a subject doesn't mean that it will appear on the paper. You will get no marks for answering questions which aren't set.

Open book examinations

If you have an open book examination you will be allowed to take certain materials into the examination room. This may be your lecture notes, handouts and a textbook. Check before hand which materials are permitted.

Don't leave revision for open book examinations until the last minute. You will still need to revise. The materials that you take into the examination should merely be an aid to your previous revision and will enable you to be accurate in your answers. Your examiner will probably expect a higher standard of answer and probably more detail if it is an open book examination.

Crucial tip	If for some reason you miss an examination, make sure you notify the appropriate person as soon as possible. Your course handbook will probably tell you what you should do. Remember if you miss an examination without good reason you could have your marks capped if you have to resit.

Useful Web sites

- Acts of Parliament   www.hmso.gov.uk/acts.htm
- Companies House   www.companies-house.gov.uk
- The Court Service   www.courtservice.gov.uk
- The Crown Prosecution Service   www.cps.gov.uk
- Findlaw (lists legal journals)   www.findlaw.com
- Government Information site   www.ukonline.gov.uk

- Law Commission — www.lawcom.gov.uk/homepage.htm
- Law Dictionary — www.duhaime.org/diction.htm
- The Lawyer — www.the-lawyer.co.uk
- Lord Chancellor's Department — www.open.gov.uk/lcd
- Parliament site — www.parliament.uk
- Statutory Instruments — www.hmso.gov.uk/stat.htm

Crucial tip — Some of these sites, for example the Government Information site, will give you a gateway to a number of other useful sites such as government departments and parliamentary sites.

Crucial tip — Your institution's library may have a subscription to a number of other Internet sites such as Lawtel and Current Legal Information. These will provide further access to a range of legal information such as case summaries and journal articles. Check with your law librarian for advice.

CHAPTER I

THE ENGLISH
LEGAL SYSTEM

Chapter summary

This chapter describes what law is and why laws are necessary. It identifies the different ways that law can be classified, the role of the courts in the English legal system, the role of alternative dispute resolution (ADR) and the role of tribunals. It describes the main sources of law, including the law of the European Union, and how these sources are created. It also considers the impact of the Human Rights Act 1998 on the English legal system.

Studying this chapter will help you to:

- understand the purpose of law and identify the different ways in which it can be classified;

- recognise the different criminal and civil courts and the type of actions that will be heard in them and understand the role of ADR and the role of tribunals;

- identify the main sources of English law and how they are created;

- understand the impact of the Human Rights Act 1998 on the English legal system.

Assessment targets

Target 1: classifying law
You must be able to describe the different ways in which law can be classified. Exercise 1 at the end of this chapter will check whether you can do this.

Target 2: court jurisdiction
You will be asked to consider in which type of court a particular case will be heard. Exercise 2 at the end of this chapter will check whether you can do this.

Target 3: sources of English law
You will be asked to outline the main sources of English law and you must understand the meaning of key terms associated with these sources. Exercise 3 at the end of this chapter will check whether you can do this.

Target 4: the Human Rights Act
You have to understand what impact the Human Rights Act 1988 has had on the English legal system. Exercise 4 at the end of this chapter will check whether you can do this.

Crucial terms, cases and Acts

What is law?
Classification of law
Burden and standard of proof
Criminal and civil courts
Alternative Dispute Resolution (ADR)
Tribunals
The main sources of English law
The rules of statutory
    interpretation

Ratio decidendi and *obiter dicta*
The main institutions of the
    European Union
Types of European law
The doctrine of parliamentary
    sovereignty
The European Court of Human
    Rights

Relevant links

The law of tort will feature in **Chapter 4**. The law of contract will feature in **Chapter 2**. Employment law will feature in **Chapter 7**.

Section 1	Introduction to law

What are you studying?
This section describes what law is and identifies the main ways in which it can be classified. It outlines who the parties are in both a civil and a criminal action and describes who has to prove the case and to what standard, in both criminal and civil proceedings.

How will you be assessed on this?
You will need to know the differences between civil and criminal law, who would bring an action in either case and to what standard they must prove their case in order to be successful.

> **Crucial concept** **What is law?** The law is a body of rules designed to regulate the way we behave in society. The rules are created by the State and are enforced through the courts. The law governs all aspects of our personal, social and business life. For example, there are laws which relate to marriage, divorce and care of children, laws which govern how we behave in public and laws covering the setting up of companies and employment of individuals.

Classification of law

> **Crucial concept** **Law** can be classified in a number of ways. These are:
> - public and private law;
> - common law and equity;
> - criminal and civil law.

PUBLIC AND PRIVATE LAW

Public law covers *constitutional law*, which is law governing the British constitution such as the reform of the House of Lords, *administrative law* which covers disputes with government agencies and *criminal law* which is described in more detail below.

Private law concerns disputes between individuals. It is also referred to as civil law. An example of civil law is the law of contract.

COMMON LAW AND EQUITY

Common law and equity developed in mediaeval times. Common law was law that was common throughout England and its principles were established and followed by the courts in similar later cases. Common law principles are still in use in the courts today. An example of common law is the law of tort.

Equity is a body of rules and principles that developed to remedy the defects in the common law. Equitable principles are based on fairness and they are still influential today in areas such as land law.

In this book we concentrate on the third classification — criminal and civil law.

CRIMINAL AND CIVIL LAW

Criminal law

Criminal law covers behaviour which is considered to be so serious and prejudicial to society that the State (the prosecution) brings an action on behalf of the Crown, against an individual or corporation (the defendant) thought to be responsible for that behaviour. Examples of criminal offences include murder, theft, rape, assault and criminal damage. It is the police who will investigate the crime initially and the Crown Prosecution Service who will prepare the case and decide whether or not to take it to court. The victim will have no say in the decision to prosecute, although it may be possible for the victim to bring his own private prosecution.

The defendant will be tried in a criminal court. It is up to the Crown Prosecution Service to prove its case *beyond reasonable doubt*. This means that those responsible for judging the defendant must be sure of his guilt. If the defendant is found guilty he will be sentenced. He may be sent to prison, he may be fined, he may be subject to a community punishment order or community rehabilitation. If the defendant is found not guilty then he will be acquitted and will be free to leave the court.

Civil law

In civil law one individual brings an action against another for some sort of wrongdoing which has resulted in injury or damage to the first individual. The person who brings the action is called the claimant and the person it is brought against is called the defendant. The case will be heard in a civil court. Examples of civil law include tort, contract and family law. The claimant has to prove his case *on the balance of probabilities*. This means that he must prove that it is more probable than not that the defendant is liable. If the defendant is found liable he will usually be required to pay damages. He may also be required to take action to stop the wrongdoing from continuing.

Crucial tip	If a case is written as *R* v *Heenan*, this will be a criminal case. 'R' stands for Regina or the Crown and 'Heenan' is the name of the defendant.
	If a case is written as *Heenan* v *Moore*, this will usually be a civil case. 'Heenan' is the name of the claimant who is bringing a claim against 'Moore', the defendant.

Crucial tip	In criminal cases the defendant may be found guilty or not guilty. In civil cases the defendant may be found liable or not liable.
	In criminal cases the prosecution brings an action against the defendant. In civil cases the claimant brings a claim against the defendant.

Crucial concept	**Burden and standard of proof.** In criminal cases the burden of proof is on the prosecution. It must prove its case beyond reasonable doubt. In civil cases the burden of proof is on the claimant to prove his case on the balance of probabilities. The standard of proof is higher in a criminal case because of the stigma attached to criminal offences and because the penalty for being found guilty of a criminal offence is potentially much greater than the penalty for being found liable in a civil case.

Quick test

Who has to prove the case and to what standard in:

- A civil case?
- A criminal case?

Section 2 — The structure of the courts

What are you studying?

This section describes the civil and criminal courts and the role that they play within the English legal system. It also describes the role of Alternative Dispute Resolution (ADR) and tribunals.

How will you be assessed on this?

You will need to understand the differences between these courts and know in which of them a particular case will be heard. You will also need to know when ADR or the use of a tribunal may be appropriate.

Criminal and civil courts

Crucial concept Courts in England are divided into criminal courts and civil courts.

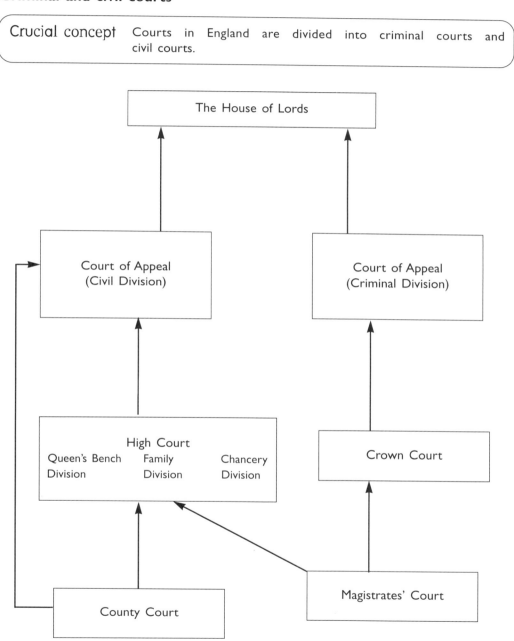

Figure 1.1 The structure of the courts in England and Wales

THE CRIMINAL COURTS

All criminal cases are initiated in the *Magistrates' Court*. The cases are usually heard by a bench of three lay magistrates who are not legally-qualified or by a single, legally-qualified District Judge. These judges were formerly known as stipendiary magistrates. Lay magistrates are assisted by a legally-qualified court clerk who is able to advise them on the law.

> **Crucial tip**   Lay magistrates are also referred to as Justices of the Peace or JPs

Criminal offences may be classified as *summary* offences (which are the least serious offences), for example minor traffic offences, *either-way* offences (for example more serious theft offences) or *indictable* offences, which are the most serious (for example rape and murder). The magistrates will try summary offences and some either-way offences but indictable offences will be tried before a judge and jury in the *Crown Court*. In some cases the magistrates will decide whether the defendant is guilty and then pass the case to the Crown Court for sentencing if they consider that the sentence to be imposed exceeds their sentencing powers. The maximum sentence that can be imposed in the Magistrates' Court is six months' imprisonment for a single offence or a fine of £5,000.

A person found guilty of an offence and sentenced in the Magistrates' Court may appeal against that sentence to the Crown Court. When a case is tried in the Crown Court, the jury will decide the facts of the case and the guilt or innocence of the defendant. The judge will decide the law and will pass sentence. Cases are normally heard before a Circuit Judge but a High Court judge will hear the more serious cases.

The criminal division of the *Court of Appeal* hears appeals from trials in the Crown Court. The appeal will be heard before a bench of three to five appeal judges, the Lord Justices of Appeal. Appeals from the Court of Appeal, are heard in the *House of Lords* before the Lords of Appeal in Ordinary, otherwise known as the Law Lords. For most cases there will be five Law Lords sitting but there may be seven for more important cases.

> **Crucial tip**   The House of Lords hears cases which are of major public importance. You cannot have your case heard by the House of Lords just because you want to.

THE CIVIL COURTS

Some civil cases are heard in the Magistrates' Court, for example some public health matters and some family proceedings.

The *County Court* and the *High Court* hear similar types of civil cases. In general a claim with a higher value will be heard in the High Court, although there may be other reasons, such as the complexity of the case, which determine the choice of court.

Claims to the County Court will be allocated to one of three tracks: the small claims track, the fast track or the multi-track. The small claims track is for uncomplicated claims of up to £5,000. The case will be heard before a District Judge. The setting will be informal and the use of lawyers is discouraged. The fast track is for claims between £5,000 and £15,000 and the length of the trial is limited to one day. The multi-track is for more complex cases involving claims of more than £15,000.

The High Court has three divisions: the Queen's Bench Division deals with matters such as contract and tort; the Family Division deals with matrimonial cases and cases involving children; and the Chancery Division deals with tax, corporate and some property matters. These cases are generally heard before one High Court judge. The High Court may also hear appeals from the County Court and the Magistrates' Court. Appeals will generally be before two or three judges.

The civil division of the *Court of Appeal* hears appeals from the High Court and the County Court. The appeal will be heard by a minimum of two Lord Justices' of Appeal.

As described above, appeals from the Court of Appeal are heard by the House of Lords. The bulk of appeals to the House of Lords concern civil matters.

> **Crucial tip**   Criminal cases are tried in the Magistrates' Court and the Crown Court. Criminal appeals may be heard in the Crown Court, the Court of Appeal and the House of Lords. Civil cases are tried in the County Court and the High Court. Civil appeals may be heard in the High Court, the Court of Appeal and the House of Lords.

Alternative Dispute Resolution (ADR)

> **Crucial concept**   **Alternative Dispute Resolution** (ADR) can be used to solve a dispute without having to go to court.

The main advantages of ADR are that it is a much cheaper and quicker alternative to court proceedings. In addition, the procedure is less complicated and more informal. The main types of ADR are:

- arbitration;

- mediation;

- conciliation.

ARBITRATION
Both parties agree that their claim will be heard before an arbitrator rather than the court and they agree to be bound by his decision. The arbitrator will have expertise in the subject matter of the dispute. Arbitration is commonly used for commercial disputes between businesses.

MEDIATION
Mediation is a method by which the parties meet and resolve the dispute themselves assisted by a mediator who is a neutral party. This method of dispute resolution may be used to resolve financial affairs following divorce.

CONCILIATION
Conciliation is favoured in employment disputes. A conciliator helps employers and employees to resolve disputes which arise between them. If conciliation fails, the parties may have to take their case to an employment tribunal.

The Advisory, Conciliation and Arbitration Service (ACAS) is a body which provides such a service with a high degree of success.

Tribunals

> **Crucial concept**   **Tribunals.** Bodies appointed to adjudicate in specific areas of law. Tribunals are set up by statute and operate outside the usual judicial hierarchy.

Tribunals provide another means of resolving a dispute. There are a number of different types of tribunal each dealing with a specialist area, for example the Employment Appeal Tribunal, the Social Security Appeal Tribunal and the Immigration Appeal Tribunal. Each tribunal normally consists of three members who have relevant expertise. The chair of the tribunal will be legally qualified.

The advantages of using tribunals are that they are cheaper, usually less formal and a case is likely to be heard relatively quickly. However, public funding (previously 'legal aid') is not available and there are criticisms of the appeals procedure. From some tribunals, appeals may be made to the ordinary courts but from others appeals may only be made to the relevant government minister who may have been responsible for implementing the rules which are the subject of the appeal, for example immigration appeals.

Quick test

1. In which courts will a civil trial take place?
2. In which courts will a criminal trial take place?
3. What is the role of ADR and the tribunals in the English legal system?

Section 3   Sources of English law

What are you studying?
This section identifies the main sources of English law. It covers the methods that the courts use for interpreting Acts of Parliament and the doctrine of judicial precedent. It also discusses the role and the main types of European law and the major institutions within the European Union. In addition, it describes the doctrine of parliamentary sovereignty.

How will you be assessed on this?
You will need to know the four main sources of English law and how these sources are created. You must be able to explain the role of statutory interpretation, the doctrine of judicial precedent and the doctrine of parliamentary sovereignty. You must also know the main sources of European law and the role of the four main institutions of the European Union.

The main sources of English law

Crucial concept   English law comes from the following main sources:
- Acts of Parliament;
- delegated legislation;
- case law;
- European law.

ACTS OF PARLIAMENT
An Act of Parliament consists of law created by Parliament. Examples include the Unfair Contract Terms Act 1977 and the Sale of Goods Act 1979. Parliament is made up of two houses: the House of Commons where elected members of Parliament (MPs) sit and the House of Lords where the non-elected members, the Lords, sit. In order for an Act to become law it has to go through a number of different parliamentary stages. Both Houses will be involved in this process. When an Act is going through these stages it is called a Bill. A Bill

may be either a public Bill or a private Bill. A public Bill is the most common type and will have been sponsored by the government. A private Bill will usually have been sponsored by a local authority and will concern changes of law applicable to that authority alone and not the country as a whole. A Private Member's Bill is a Bill introduced by a member of one of the Houses. It usually concerns moral issues which are not always supported by the government. There is a limited amount of parliamentary time available to debate Private Member's Bills and so they rarely become law.

The stages that the Bill goes through before it becomes an Act of Parliament are as follows:

- **First Reading.** The Bill is formally notified to the House.

- **Second Reading.** There is a debate and vote on the Bill.

- **Committee Stage.** If the vote has been successful, there will be a detailed discussion of the Bill by a Standing Committee who will propose any necessary amendments. A Standing Committee is made up of MPs, some of whom may have expertise of the subject matter of the Bill.

- **Report Stage.** The Bill is amended and the House considers the amendments.

- **Third Reading.** There is a further debate and verbal amendments are allowed.

- **House of Lords.** The Bill is passed to the other House where it goes through a similar process. This will usually be the House of Lords but if the Bill commenced its passage in the House of Lords it will pass to the House of Commons at this stage.

- **Royal Assent.** The Queen gives her approval to the Bill. This is a formality and her approval is never refused. The Bill now becomes an Act of Parliament.

> Crucial tip   A statute is another name for an Act of Parliament.

How are Acts of Parliament interpreted by the courts?

If the language contained within the Act is not immediately clear, the judge may use one of a number of rules to interpret the wording. Initially the judge may look at the Act itself which may define the meaning of certain words. The judge may also refer to other sources such as the Interpretation Act 1978, reports to the Law Commission, and *Hansard* which contains reports of parliamentary proceedings to see what discussion took place before the Act was passed.

> Crucial concept   **Rules of statutory interpretation.** These are defined by the literal rule, the golden rule, the mischief rule and the *ejusdem generis* rule.

The literal rule

The words in the statute are given their ordinary literal meaning, provided that there is no ambiguity. An example of this rule is the case of *IRC v Hinchy* (1960). The penalty under statute for incorrectly completing a tax return was 'treble the tax that ought to be charged'. The court interpreted this as three times the tax bill for the year rather than three times the amount owed which was what the defendant had presumed was payable.

The golden rule

If the literal rule would give an absurd meaning to the words, they are interpreted in a way that overcomes this absurdity. An example of this rule can be found in the case of *Re Sigsworth*

(1935). A man who murdered his mother could not benefit from her estate as it is a principle of law that you cannot benefit from your own wrongdoing.

The mischief rule

The court will consider what purpose Parliament had in mind when it passed the Act and will interpret the wording in line with this purpose. An example is the case of *Gardiner* v *Sevenoaks RDC* (1950). A man kept his film in a cave and because of this he claimed that he was not bound by law concerning the storage of film in premises. The court held that the cave should be classified as premises. It looked at Parliament's purpose in passing the legislation which was to protect those who lived nearby or who worked on the premises.

The *ejusdem generis* rule

If two or more specific words are followed by a general word, that general word will be interpreted in the same way as the specific word. For example, whiskey, brandy and other drinks would probably include vodka but not orange squash.

DELEGATED LEGISLATION

As Parliamentary time is limited and because of a lack of expertise, it is not always possible to create all the legislation that is required. In order to overcome this problem, Parliament delegates authority to other bodies to draw up the additional legislation. The main types of delegated legislation are:

- **Orders in Council** which are made by members of the Privy Council (usually cabinet ministers). They are used for emergency measures and Commonwealth issues.

- **Statutory instruments** which are regulations made by government departments in respect of that department. For example, social security rules.

- **Bye-laws** which are drafted by local authorities and other public bodies to govern the way they run their activities. For example, rules preventing skateboarding in city centres and shopping malls.

CASE LAW

Some areas of law are not covered by Acts of Parliament or delegated legislation. Under these circumstances the court may need to refer to and follow the decisions made by other courts in previous similar cases. This is known as the doctrine of judicial precedent. Not all courts are bound to follow the previous decisions of other courts:

- Decisions made by the House of Lords are binding on all courts beneath it. It does not have to follow the decisions of those courts and it does not have to follow its own previous decisions.

- Decisions made by the Court of Appeal are binding on courts below it but not on the House of Lords. With limited exceptions it is bound to follow its own decisions.

- Decisions made in the High Court are binding on the lower courts and it is bound by the decisions of courts above it.

- Decisions made by the Crown Court, the Magistrates' Court and the County Court are not binding on the other courts although these courts are bound by the decisions of the courts above them.

> **Crucial concept** ***Ratio decidendi*** **and *obiter dicta*.** At the end of a case the judge or judges will sum up and give a judgment. The part of the judgment that must be followed is called the *ratio decidendi*, meaning the reason for the decision. Other parts of the judgment may be persuasive and future courts, although not obliged to, may decide to follow them. These parts are called the *obiter dicta*, meaning things said by the way.

A judge is not bound to follow a previous decision if he can distinguish the facts of the present case from the facts of the previous case.

EUROPEAN LAW

Since the United Kingdom joined the European Economic Community (now referred to as the European Union) in 1973 and enacted the European Communities Act 1972, it has been bound by its law. Where there is a conflict between English law and EU law, the latter will prevail and any disputes must be referred to the European Court of Justice in Luxembourg.

The European Court is one of the four main institutions of the EU, the others being the European Parliament, the European Commission and the Council of Ministers.

> **Crucial concept** The four main institutions of the EU are the European Court of Justice, the European Parliament, the European Commission and the Council of Ministers.

The European Court of Justice

The court is made up of 15 judges who are assisted by nine Advocates-General. The role of an Advocate-General is to summarise the facts of a case and make a recommendation to the court about what the outcome of the case should be. They must act with complete impartiality and independence. There is no obligation for the court to follow their recommendation.

The main functions of the court are as follows:

- to give a preliminary ruling on the interpretation of EU law;

- to hear cases against Member States and community institutions who have not fulfilled their obligations under EU law;

- to hear disputes between EU institutions and their employees.

> **Crucial tip** The European Court of Justice is quite separate from the European Court of Human Rights which is discussed in more detail in Section 4 of this chapter.

The European Parliament

Members of the European Parliament (MEP's) are elected every five years by the electorate within their own State. Each of the 15 Member States contains a number of constituencies and from each of these an MEP is elected. Unlike our own Members of Parliament, they play a minor role in the legislative process. However, they have the power to dismiss the Commission and to reject the EU budget.

The European Commission

This consists of 20 Commissioners nominated by the governments of Member States. The larger States nominate two Commissioners and the smaller States nominate one. The Commissioners must act independently of their own government and in the best interests of the EU. Their role is to propose and implement legislation and ensure that Member States meet certain legal obligations such as enforcing directives.

The Council of Ministers

This is composed of a Minister from each Member State who will vary depending on the topic being discussed. Its main role is to consider whether the proposals made by the Commission should be implemented. Sometimes it is Prime Ministers and leaders of each government who meet to discuss crucial issues, for example, enlarging the EU.

> Crucial concept　**Types of European law.** European law comes from the following sources: treaties, regulations, directives and decisions.

- **Treaties.** These are major sources of EU law which are binding on all Members States. In the UK an Act of Parliament is required to give effect to the Treaty.

- **Regulations.** Regulations are binding in all the Member States as soon as they are issued. Their purpose is to achieve uniformity of law throughout the EU. They are the equivalent of an Act of Parliament in the UK.

- **Directives.** Directives are also designed to achieve uniformity of law throughout Member States. They do not have immediate effect, although Member States are required to implement them within a given timescale. If the Member State fails to comply, sanctions may be brought against that State.

- **Decisions.** A decision may be addressed to a Member State, an organisation or an individual and will be binding on them.

> Crucial concept　**The doctrine of Parliamentary sovereignty.** By being a member of the European Union, the UK is bound by EU law and as a result our own Parliament is no longer supreme. However, the situation could be reversed if a decision was made to leave the EU. To do this Parliament would need to repeal the European Communities Act 1972. This option does seem unlikely today in view of the ever-increasing close economic ties that the UK has with Europe.

Quick test

1. What are the main sources of English law?
2. Identify the four main institutions of the EU.

What are you studying?
This section outlines the main provisions of the Human Rights Act 1998 and describes the role of the European Court of Human Rights.

How you will be assessed on this?
You will need to know the main provisions of the 1998 Act and the impact that it has had on the English legal system.

The Human Rights Act 1998 came into force on 2 October 2000. It incorporates the European Convention on Human Rights into the English legal system. The Convention was originally drawn up after the Second World War with the aim of protecting the human rights of people in Europe following the abuses that occurred during that war. Since the Human Rights Act 1998 came into force, these rights are now enforceable in English courts. Rights are protected by means of a number of Articles and Protocols contained within the Convention. The most important of these are listed in Figure 1.2 below.

Article 2	Right to life
Article 3	Prohibition of torture
Article 4	Prohibition of slavery and forced labour
Article 5	Right to liberty and security
Article 6	Right to a fair trial
Article 7	No punishment without lawful authority
Article 8	Right to respect for family and private life
Article 9	Freedom of thought, conscience and religion
Article 10	Freedom of expression
Article 11	Freedom of assembly and association
Article 12	Right to marry
Article 13	Right to an effective remedy
Article 14	Prohibition of discrimination
The First Protocol, Article 1	Protection of property
The First Protocol, Article 2	Right to education
The First Protocol, Article 3	Free elections

Figure 1.2 Rights protected by the European Convention on Human Rights

Individuals may bring an action against public bodies which can include the courts, public organisations, eg the NHS and private organisations acting in a public capacity eg railway companies. These public bodies must act in a way which is compatible with the Convention and the courts must interpret legislation to be compatible with these rights. If the higher courts, which excludes the County Court, the Magistrates' Court and the Crown Court, are unable to do this they may make a declaration of incompatibility. Such a declaration may make the government consider whether to change the relevant law. When new legislation comes into force it should as far as it is possible be compatible with the Convention rights.

The courts must also take into account any previous relevant case-law from the European Court of Human Rights and give effect to it.

The European Court of Human Rights. The European Court of Human Rights is based in Strasbourg and is totally separate from the European Court of Justice. Before the introduction of the Human Rights Act 1998, the only remedy for an individual who felt that his Convention rights had being breached by the State, was to bring an action in the European Court of Human Rights. Today the individual must bring his case in the English courts and he may only bring a case before the European Court of Human Rights if all avenues have been exhausted in the home courts. The decisions of the European Court are binding on the State to which they are addressed, although they cannot be enforced.

Quick test

What is the role of the European Court of Human Rights?

Crucial examples

These questions relate to the assessment targets set out at the beginning of this chapter.

1. (a) In what ways can law be classified?
    (b) Describe the main differences between civil and criminal law.

2. In which courts will the following cases be heard?
    (a) A trial for exceeding the speed limit.
    (b) A trial for rape.
    (c) An appeal against a conviction for murder.
    (d) A claim for a breach of contract with a value of £3,000.
    (e) A claim for unfair dismissal.

3. (a) What are the main sources of English law?
    (b) Explain what is meant by the following:
    - Royal Assent;
    - the literal rule;
    - *ratio decidendi*;
    - *obiter dicta*.

4. (a) What impact has the Human Rights Act 1998 had on the English legal system?

Answers

1. (a) You will need to state that law can be classified in a number of ways. These are as public and private law, as common law and equity and civil and criminal law. You would need to give a brief description of each of these as contained within Section 1 of this chapter.
    (b) The main differences between civil and criminal law are as follows:
    - In a criminal case the action is brought by the prosecution against the defendant who will be punished if he is found guilty of a wrongful act. In a civil case the

claimant brings a claim against the defendant for injury or damage caused. The purpose of the claim will usually be for damages to compensate for the loss suffered by the claimant.

- In a criminal case the burden of proof is on the prosecution to prove the case beyond reasonable doubt. In a civil case the burden of proof is on the claimant to prove the case on the balance of probabilities.

- A criminal case will be heard in one of the criminal courts, usually the Magistrates' Court or the Crown Court. A civil case will generally be heard in the County Court or the High Court.

- In a criminal case the defendant will be found guilty or not guilty. In a civil case the defendant will be either liable or not liable.

2. (a) The Magistrates' Court.
   (b) The Crown Court.
   (c) The Court of Appeal (Criminal Division).
   (d) The County Court (small claims track).
   (e) The employment tribunal.

3. (a) The four main sources of English law are:
   - Acts of Parliament;

   - delegated legislation;

   - case law;

   - European law;

   You would need to be able to give a description of these. This can be found in Section 3 of this chapter.
   (b) Royal Assent is when the Queen gives her approval to a bill. The bill then becomes an Act of Parliament.

   The literal rule is one of the rules that can be used by a judge when he is interpreting the wording of an Act of Parliament. Under this rule the judge would give the words their ordinary literal meaning.

   The *ratio decidendi* of a case is the part of the judgment which forms the binding precedent for future cases.

   The *obiter dicta* is the part of the judgement which is not binding precedent but may be persuasive in future cases.

4. The rights contained within the European Convention on Human Rights are now enforceable in the English courts. Public authorities and the courts must now act in a way which is compatible with those rights. Legislation must be interpreted to be compatible with those rights and the courts must give effect to case law from the European Court of Human Rights.

Crucial reading and research

Holland and Webb, *Learning Legal Rules*, 4th edn., Oxford.

Parlington, *Introduction to the English Legal System*, Oxford.

Slapper and Kelly, *The English Legal System* 5th edn., Cavendish.

Wadham and Mountford, *Blackstone's Guide to the Human Rights Act 1998*, Oxford.

CHAPTER 2

CONTRACT

Chapter summary

This chapter describes how a legally binding agreement, otherwise known as a contract is formed. It describes the terms that can be included in a contract and how parties may limit or exclude their liability. It also considers when contracts may be void or voidable and how they may come to an end.

Studying this chapter will help you to:

- understand and describe the elements which must be included in a legally binding contract;

- identify how terms are incorporated into a contract and how those terms may be classified;

- recognise how liability in contracts may be limited or excluded;

- understand the factors which make a contract void or voidable;

- understand the ways in which a contract may come to an end or be discharged and the remedies available to the innocent party when there is a breach of contract.

Assessment targets

Target 1: identifying a valid contract
You must be able to identify when a valid contract has been formed. Exercise 1 at the end of this chapter will check whether you can do this.

Target 2: identifying how terms are incorporated and classified
You must know how terms are incorporated into a contract and how they may be classified. You must also be able to identify when an exclusion clause is valid. Exercise 2 at the end of this chapter will check whether you can do this.

Target 3: understanding void and voidable contracts
You must be able to describe the factors which make a contract void or voidable. Exercise 3 at the end of this chapter will check whether you can do this.

Target 4: identifying when a contract ends
You must be able to identify when a contract comes to an end and the remedies for breach of contract. Exercise 4 at the end of this chapter will check whether you can do this.

Crucial terms, cases and Acts

What is a contract?
The offer
Fisher v Bell (1960)
Pharmaceutical Society of Great Britain v Boots Cash Chemists (1952)
Carlill v Carbolic Smoke Ball Co. Ltd (1893)
Acceptance
Consideration
A legal purpose
Capacity
Intention to create legal relations
Express terms
Implied terms
Classification of terms

Conditions
Warranties
Innominate terms
Exclusion clauses
Void and voidable contracts
Mistake
Misrepresentation
Duress
Undue influence
Performance
Agreement
Frustration
Breach
Remedies for breach of contract

Relevant links

The supply of goods and services is covered in **Chapter 3**.

Section 1 Formation of the contract

What are you studying?
This section describes what a contract is and what elements are necessary for the contract to be legally binding.

How will you be assessed on this?
In an examination you may be asked to describe the elements of a legally binding contract. You could be given a problem question and asked to identify whether a valid contract exists between two parties.

> **Crucial concept**   **What is a contract?** A contract is an agreement between two or more people (or organisations) which is binding in law.

Everyday most people make contracts, for example when they buy a bottle of milk or when they catch a bus. Both parties to the contract have obligations. One party may provide a product or a service and the other party is obliged to pay for it. If one of the parties does not fulfil his obligations then it may be possible for the other party to sue for breach of contract.

The majority of contracts do not have to be in writing. An oral agreement can be sufficient. However, some written proof of the contract, even a till receipt from a purchase or a bus ticket, is advisable to protect the parties if something goes wrong.

For a contract to be legally binding it must have the following elements:

- an offer;
- acceptance;
- consideration;
- a legal purpose;
- capacity;
- intention to be legally bound.

The offer

> **Crucial concept**   An **offer** is made when a person sets out terms on which he is prepared to do business. The terms of the contract must be clear and capable of being accepted. It is the offeror who makes the offer to the offeree.

> **Crucial tip**   Either the buyer or the seller may be offeror. For example, if A says to B, 'Would you like to buy my car for £4,000?', then A is the offeror and B is the offeree. If B says to A, 'I would like to buy your car for £4,000', then B is the offeror and A is the offeree.

There are two main types of offer – bilateral and unilateral. *Bilateral offers* are the most common and they are made when a person makes a promise in return for a promise. For example, 'If you clean my car I will give you £5'. *Unilateral offers* are when a person makes an offer but is not certain whether it will be accepted. They are often made to a number of people at the same time and they amount to a promise in return for an act. A reward advertised for finding a lost pet is an example. It is made to anyone willing to look for the animal but is only capable of being accepted by the person finding it.

Offers must be clearly distinguished from:

- an invitation to treat;
- a counter offer;
- a request for information.

Invitation to treat

An invitation to treat is sometimes confused with an offer. In effect it is the stage before the offer and it amounts to an enticement to make an offer.

> **Crucial tip** An invitation to treat does not form part of the contract.

Goods for sale in a shop window or on a shop shelf will be regarded as an invitation to treat and not an offer for sale.

> **Crucial case** **Fisher v Bell (1960).** A flick knife with a price ticket attached was displayed in a shop window. The court held that this amounted to an invitation to treat and not an offer for sale.

> **Crucial case** **Pharmaceutical Society of Great Britain v Boots Cash Chemists (1952).** A display of goods on a shop shelf was held to be an invitation to treat. The offer was made when the customer took the goods to the cash till.

Advertisements

Generally an advertisement will be regarded as an invitation to treat. However in certain cases the advertisement may be a unilateral offer.

> **Crucial case** **Carlill v Carbolic Smoke Ball Co. Ltd (1893).** An advertisement was placed in a newspaper. It stated that anyone who used the company's smokeball correctly and then contracted influenza would be entitled to £100. Mrs Carlill caught influenza after using the smokeball and tried to claim £100. The company argued that the advertisement was not an offer and she was not entitled to claim. The court disagreed and stated that it was a unilateral offer to the world at large. The company had placed £100 with their bankers which was evidence that they intended to be bound by their promise.

Counter offer

A counter offer occurs when the offeree tries to change the terms of the offer after it has been made. For example, A may offer his car for sale to B for £5,000 and B replies by saying that he will buy it for £4,500. B's reply is a counter offer and it destroys the original offer. B cannot then accept A's original offer as it no longer exists. It is up to A to accept or reject B's counter offer.

If B decides that he is prepared to pay £5,000 for the car, he must make a new offer to A which A may decide to accept or reject.

Request for information

This should not be confused with an offer or a counter offer. It is merely a request for more information about the item being sold. For example, A may offer his car to B. B then asks whether the radio is included in the sale.

How offers come to an end

An offer may come to an end in one of the following ways:

- revocation;

- lapse of time;

- termination by the offeree.

REVOCATION

The offer may be withdrawn at anytime before it is accepted. Notice of the withdrawal must be communicated to the offeree. It does not matter who gives notice of the revocation. It need not be the offeror.

Example: Dickenson v Dodds (1876)
The offeror offered to sell a house to the offeree and gave him two days to accept. In the meantime the offeror sold the house to another. A mutual friend told the offeree of the sale and he immediately tried to accept the initial offer. It was held that he could not do this as he had been notified of the revocation.

> **Crucial tip**   A promise to keep an offer open for a period of time is unlikely to be binding on the offeror unless the offeree has given something in return, such as a deposit. For example, if B is selling a car and A asks him to hold the car until Friday, B is not obliged to do so unless A gives something, such as a deposit, for B's promise.

LAPSE OF TIME

If the offer has been kept open for a specific time period, it will automatically come to an end when that time period ends unless it has been accepted. Other offers will remain open for a reasonable time.

Example: Ramsgate Victoria Hotel Co. v Montfiore (1866)
In June the defendant made an offer to buy shares in the claimant's company. He heard nothing until November when he was asked to pay for the shares. It was held that as the offer had not been accepted within a reasonable amount of time he was not bound to pay for the shares.

TERMINATION BY THE OFFEREE

The offeree may reject the offer or make a counter offer, in which case the offer comes to an end.

Acceptance

> **Crucial concept**   **Acceptance.** The offeree must accept the offer on exactly the same terms as it is offered and this must be communicated to the offeror by an authorised person. Any attempt to vary the terms will result in a new offer being made. Acceptance may be made by conduct, writing or words.

Generally the contract will not be formed until acceptance is received by the offeror. However, there are special rules which apply when acceptance is by post.

THE POSTAL RULE

When acceptance is by post it is effective as soon as it is posted as long as it has been correctly addressed.

Example: Adams v *Lindsell* (1818)

This case established the postal rule, that a correctly addressed letter of acceptance is valid as soon as it is posted.

Crucial tip	Note that letters containing offers and revocation of offers are valid when they are received. Letters containing acceptance of an offer are valid when they are posted.

A sensible businessman would not make a contract which relied on acceptance by post.

AUCTIONS

At auction, the bidder makes an offer which is accepted by the auctioneer on the fall of the hammer.

Consideration

Crucial concept	**Consideration.** To have a valid contract, each party must give something to the other. This is known as consideration. For example, A makes a promise to sell a car and B makes a promise to pay for the car.

Consideration may be *executory*, which is a promise to do something in the future or *executed* which is when one party makes an offer or a promise and it is up to the other party to perform an act before the contract is complete. (Like a reward for finding a lost pet.)

There are certain rules which relate to consideration:

- consideration must move from the promisee;
- past consideration is no consideration;
- consideration must be sufficient but need not be adequate.

CONSIDERATION MUST MOVE FROM THE PROMISEE

If C pays D £25 for flowers to be delivered to E, then under most circumstances E cannot enforce the contract because she is not a party to it and has provided no consideration. This ties in with the rule of *privity of contract* which states that in most cases only parties to the contract can sue and be sued on it. However since the *Contracts (Rights of Third Parties) Act 1999* became law it is now possible in some cases for a third party to enforce a contractual term.

PAST CONSIDERATION IS NO CONSIDERATION

After an action has been performed, a promise in relation to that action is not contractually enforceable. For example, if B cleans A's car and afterwards A offers to pay B £5, that promise cannot be enforced by B if A refuses to pay.

CONSIDERATION MUST BE SUFFICIENT BUT NEED NOT BE ADEQUATE

Consideration must have some value but it need not be the true economic value.

Example: Thomas v *Thomas* (1842)
A widow was allowed to remain in her dead husband's house for the sum of £1 per year. This was held to be sufficient consideration.

Promissory estoppel

In *Pinnel's Case* (1602) a rule was established which stated that if a debtor made a part payment of a debt and the creditor accepted this payment as full settlement, the creditor may still sue for the remainder of the debt. This appears to go against the rule that consideration must be sufficient but need not be adequate and seems to be unfair to the person who believed they had settled their debt.

The doctrine of promissory estoppel helps overcome the harshness of this rule. It prevents a person who has made a promise from breaking that promise if the court feels it would be unfair to allow him to do so. The doctrine was developed in the case of *Central London Property Trust Ltd* v *High Trees House Ltd* (1947).

A good example of the rule in application is the case of *Williams* v *Roffey Bros* (1990). Williams was subcontracted as a carpenter for work on a block of flats. Part of the way through the job he realised that the price he had quoted was uneconomical and he told the defendants that he was unable to complete. They verbally agreed to pay him extra in order to avoid a penalty clause which would be payable if they did not complete the job on time. He completed the work on eight more flats but received no extra payment. He sued the defendants for damages and was successful. The defendants had received the benefit of avoiding a penalty clause in return for the extra payment and this constituted sufficient extra consideration.

A legal purpose

Crucial concept	**A legal purpose.** The subject of the contract must be legal. Any contract for sexual purposes, criminal offences or civil wrongs will be unlawful.

Capacity

Crucial concept	**Capacity.** The parties must have the capacity to enter into the contract.

Certain categories of people are regarded as not having capacity:

- minors;
- those of unsound mind;
- those who are intoxicated.

MINORS

A minor is a person aged under 18. A contract that the minor makes for necessaries, such as food and clothing, will be valid and enforceable. Any other contract that the minor makes is voidable if he chooses to repudiate it while still a minor.

Crucial tip	It doesn't mean that a minor can buy things and keep them without paying for them. If he doesn't honour the contract, goods can still be recovered.

THOSE OF UNSOUND MIND/ THOSE WHO ARE INTOXICATED

A person of unsound mind or who is intoxicated may avoid the contract if it can be shown that at the time of making the contract his mind was so affected that he was not aware of what he was doing and the other party knew or should have known of this.

Intention to be legally bound

> Crucial concept The presumption of an intention to create legal relations depends on the type of agreement being made.

COMMERCIAL AND BUSINESS AGREEMENTS

It will be presumed that those who make a commercial or business agreement intend to be legally bound by that agreement unless they indicate to the contrary.

Example: *Jones* v *Vernon's Pools Ltd* (1938)
The pools company denied that they had received Mr Jones' winning coupon. They were successful in claiming that the clause in the coupon, 'binding in honour only', meant that there was no legally binding contract between the parties.

SOCIAL AND DOMESTIC AGREEMENTS

It will be presumed that family and friends who enter into an agreement do not intend to be legally bound by it unless they indicate to the contrary.

Example: *Merritt* v *Merritt* (1970)
A husband agreed to pay his estranged wife £40 per month in return for her paying the mortgage. He agreed to transfer the house to her when the mortgage was paid off. He later refused to do this. The court held there was intention to create legal relations and there was a binding contract. Their domestic relationship having broken down this was not a mere domestic agreement.

Quick test

1. Explain the difference between an offer and an invitation to treat.
2. What is meant by consideration?
3. Explain the doctrine of promissory estoppel.

Section 2	**Contractual terms**

What are you studying?
This section describes how terms are incorporated into a contract and how terms may be classified. It also describes how parties to a contract seek to limit or exclude their liability under the contract.

How will you be assessed on this?
You will need to know how terms are incorporated into the contract and how they can be classified. You must also be able to identify whether an exclusion clause is valid or otherwise. Problem questions featuring exclusion clauses are quite popular and can be combined with sale of goods issues when sellers' attempt to introduce exclusion clauses into sale of goods contracts.

Incorporation of terms

> Crucial concept **Express and implied terms.** Terms can be expressed or implied into the contract.

EXPRESS TERMS

Express terms are terms which are agreed between the parties. They may be written, spoken or a mixture of the two.

IMPLIED TERMS

Terms which have not specifically been agreed between the parties may be implied into the contract in a number of ways:

- by statute;
- by common law;
- by custom.

By statute

Certain statutes will imply terms into the contract. An example is the *Sale of Goods Act 1979*. An implied term contained within s. 14 states that goods sold in the course of a business must be of satisfactory quality. The Act and its other implied terms are explained in more detail in Chapter 3.

By common law

Under some circumstances the courts will imply a term into a contract after giving consideration to the intention of the parties.

Example: The Moorcock (1889)

The defendants agreed to let mooring space on their wharf for the claimant's ship. Damage was caused to the ship when it hit a rock at low tide. The defendants were held liable for the damage, as the courts implied a term into the contract that the wharf should be safe for the mooring of ships.

By custom

If a particular business practice is customary in certain trades or in certain areas of the country then that custom may be implied into the contract.

Example: Hutton v Warren (1836)

A tenant farmer was able to claim an allowance for his labour because this was customary in the area that he lived, despite there being no such express term in the lease.

Classification of terms

> Crucial concept Terms may be classified according to their importance as:
> - conditions;
> - warranties;
> - innominate.

CONDITIONS

Crucial concept	A **condition** is a major term of the contract. If a condition is broken it entitles the injured party to bring the contract to an end and claim damages.

Example: Poussard v Spiers (1876)
The claimant, an opera singer, became ill and was unable to perform for the first week of her contract. It was held that the employers were entitled to end the contract and to replace her because her failure to perform during the first week amounted to a breach of condition.

WARRANTIES

Crucial concept	A **warranty** is a minor term of the contract. If it is broken the injured party may claim damages but may not bring the contract to an end.

Example: Bettini v Gye (1876)
An opera singer arrived three days late for rehearsals. It was held that the contract could not be terminated as failure to attend rehearsals was a breach of a warranty rather than a condition.

INNOMINATE TERMS

Crucial concept	An **innominate term** is one where it is not possible to tell whether it is a condition or warranty from looking at the wording. It is only possible to tell after the term has been breached. The more serious the consequences of the breach, the more likely it is that the contract may be terminated.

Example: Hong Kong Fir Shipping Co. Ltd v Kawasaki Kisen Kaisha (1962)
A contractual term for the charter of a ship stated that the ship would be 'in every way fitted for ordinary cargo service'. The court decided that this was an innominate term. It would depend upon the consequences of the breach as to whether the contract may be brought to an end or whether only damages would be payable.

Crucial tip	Beware of one party stating in the contract that every term is a condition if there is a breach. The courts won't necessarily treat every term broken as a condition. Some terms are bound to have less significance in the contract than others and can only be warranties.

Exclusion clauses

> **Crucial concept** By inserting an **exclusion** clause into the contract, a party may seek to exclude or limit his liability when there is a breach of contract. For such a clause to be valid a number of conditions must be considered.
> - Is the clause included within the contract?
> - Does the clause cover what really happened?
> - Does the Unfair Contract Terms Act 1977 make the clause ineffective or make it subject to the test of reasonableness?
> - Does the Unfair Terms in Consumer Contracts Regulations 1999 apply?

Is the clause included within the contract?
A party must be given *notice of the clause* before the contract is formed.

Example: Olley v Marlborough Court Ltd (1949)
A couple went to stay in a hotel and paid in advance. When they went to their room there was a notice on the back of the door which stated that the hotel proprietors would not be liable for loss or theft of items unless they were given to the management for safe keeping. A thief stole some of their belongings. It was held that the hotel could not rely on the exclusion notice as the contract had been completed before they arrived in their room and the notice was not part of the contract.

If the parties have had regular *prior dealings* with each other then it is assumed that they have knowledge of the clause in later contracts. For example, in the above case if the couple had previously visited the hotel, they would have had prior knowledge of the clause and it would have been included within the contract.

If the contract is *signed* then the signatory will be bound by its terms even if he has not read them.

The clause may be overriden by an *inconsistent oral statement*.

Example: Curtis v Chemical Cleaning and Dyeing Co. (1951)
A lady took her wedding dress to be dry cleaned and was asked to sign a form which excluded the liability of the dry cleaners in case of damage to the dress. She was told that it protected the cleaners if there was any damage to the beads or sequins on the dress. When it came back the dress was badly stained. The cleaners were unable to rely on the exclusion clause as it had been overriden by the oral statement.

Does the clause cover what really happened?
If the terms of the clause are not clear or are ambiguous, the courts apply the *contra proferentum* rule. This means that they will interpret the clause in a way that is least favourable to the maker.

Example: Andrew Bros Ltd v Singer and Co. (1934)
An exclusion clause for the sale of a number of new cars stated that 'all conditions, warranties and liabilities implied by statute, common law or otherwise are excluded'. One of the cars was not new and the claimant tried to sue for breach of contract. The defendants sought to rely on the exclusion clause. The court held that it was an express term and not an implied term of the contract that the cars should be new and the claimants were successful in their claim.

Does the Unfair Contract Terms Act 1977 make the clause ineffective or make it subject to the test of reasonableness?

The Unfair Contract Terms Act 1977 applies where the contract is a business contract. This may be where two businesses have a contract or where a business has a contract with an individual consumer. It does not apply to private sales between individuals.

The main provisions of the Act regarding exclusion clauses are as follows:

- Liability cannot be excluded for death or personal injury where it is caused by negligence (s. 2(1)).

- Liability cannot be excluded for loss or damage where it is caused by negligence unless it is reasonable (s. 2(2)).

- Where a contract is entered into on one party's written standard terms, that party cannot exclude liability unless it is reasonable (s. 3).

- Under s. 6, where there is a contract for the sale of goods or for hire purchase, the implied term under the Sale of Goods Act 1979, that a seller has a right to sell (s. 12), can never be excluded. Implied terms as to description, quality, fitness for purpose and sale by sample cannot be excluded where the sale is to a consumer. In a business sale these terms can only be excluded as long as they are reasonable.

- Section 7 makes similar provisions to s. 6 where terms are excluded which are implied into the contract by the Supply of Goods and Services Act 1982.

The 1977 Act states that the clause should be fair and reasonable having regard to the circumstances which were known or ought to have been known to the parties at the time the contract was made.

Schedule 2 gives further guidelines for determining what is reasonable:

- The relative bargaining power of the parties.

- Whether one of the parties was given an unfair inducement to accept the term and whether the other party could have made a similar contract without the term.

- Whether the party had prior knowledge of the existence of the term.

- Where the term excludes or limits liability if the condition is not complied with, is compliance with the condition reasonable?

- Were the goods made as a special order for the consumer?

Does the Unfair Terms in Consumer Contracts Regulations 1999 apply?

The 1999 Regulations give effect to EC Directive 93/13. They apply to any unfair term in contracts between a business and a consumer. A consumer is an individual who is not acting in a business, trade or profession. The term must not have been individually negotiated between the parties.

It will be regarded as unfair if the term is contrary to the requirement of good faith and it causes a significant imbalance in the parties' rights and obligations arising under the contract to the detriment of the consumer. Any term found to be unfair may be rendered voidable (see Section 3).

Quick test

1. How may terms be incorporated into a contract?
2. In what ways may terms be classified?
3. What is the purpose of an exclusion clause?

Section 3   Defective contracts

What are you studying?
This section describes the factors which may make a contract void or voidable.

How will you be assessed on this?
Questions may ask a student to decide if there are factors which would make a contract void or voidable and identify the factors involved.

Void and voidable contracts

> Crucial concept   **Void and voidable contracts.** A contract may appear to be valid but certain factors may make the contract void or voidable. A void contract is one which is so flawed that it has never been valid. A voidable contract is valid until the innocent party chooses to end it.

Factors which may make a contract void or voidable are:

- mistake;
- misrepresentation;
- duress;
- undue influence.

MISTAKE

> Crucial concept   **Mistake.** If there is a mistake then the contract may be void at common law and voidable in equity.

There may be:

- common mistake;
- mutual mistake;
- unilateral mistake;
- mistake regarding signed contracts.

Common mistake
This is where both parties make the same mistake concerning the contract.

Common mistake as to the subject matter of the contract

Example: Scott v Coulson (1903)
Two parties entered into a contract for life assurance. Both parties believed that the assured person was alive when the contract was made whereas he was dead. The contract was void.

Common mistake as to who owns the goods

Example: Cooper v Phibbs (1867)
A agreed to lease a fishery from B. Neither was aware that A was already a tenant for life of the fishery and B had no title to it. The contract was voidable in equity.

Common mistake as to quality

This type of mistake is less likely to have an effect on the validity of the contract. It is usually considered to be a bad bargain.

Example: Leaf v International Galleries (1950)

The claimant bought a painting from the defendant. Both mistakenly believed it to have been painted by Constable. The contract was held not to be voidable.

> Crucial tip
>
> *Caveat emptor* – let the buyer beware. People cannot avoid contracts just because they make deals which turn out to be less advantageous to them when there is no element of fraud or deceit.

Mutual mistake

This occurs where the parties are at cross purposes.

Example: Raffles v Wichelhaus (1864)

The parties made a contract for the purchase of some cotton which was due to arrive in Liverpool from Bombay on a ship called *'the Peerless'*. There were two ships by this name, one sailing in October and one in December. The parties were at cross purposes about which ship the cotton was to arrive on. The contract was void.

Unilateral mistake

This occurs where one party makes a mistake and the other party is aware of the mistake but encourages the contract to continue.

Example: Lewis v Averay (1972)

When buying a second-hand car from the claimant, the defendant claimed to be an actor known as Richard Greene. He signed a cheque in that name and showed a pass to Pinewood studios bearing his name and photograph as proof of identity. It was held that the contract was not void as the identity of the defendant was not crucial to the contract.

Mistake regarding signed documents

If a document is signed, the parties are bound by the contents whether they have read it or not unless there has been fraud or misrepresentation, in which case the contract may be voidable. It may be possible to plead *non est factum* (this is not my deed), stating that what has been signed is not what it was believed to be. It must be shown that:

- there is a mistake as to the document signed and what the party believed they were signing (for example, if they believed they were signing a conveyance when in fact it was a mortgage);

- the signatory was not careless in signing the document.

Example: Saunders v Anglia Building Society (1970)

Mrs Gallie planned to leave her house to her nephew after her death. She signed a document which she believed to be to this effect without reading it as her glasses were broken. The document actually stated that the house was assigned to her nephew and that he had paid for it. The nephew obtained a mortgage on the house and did not meet the repayments. The Building Society tried to repossess the house. *Non est factum* could not be pleaded as there was little difference between the document she had signed and what she believed she was signing. Also she had been careless in not checking the document before signing it.

MISREPRESENTATION

> **Crucial concept**   **Misrepresentation.** A statement which is made which induces a party to enter into a contract is a representation. If it is false then it is a misrepresentation and the contract will become voidable. The innocent party may rescind the contract and/or claim damages.

> **Crucial tip**   An action for misrepresentation is not a breach of contact as it would occur before the contract was made and would not be a term of the contract.

There are three main types of misrepresentation:

- fraudulent;
- negligent;
- innocent.

Fraudulent misrepresentation

This is an untrue statement which the maker knows is not true or is made recklessly not caring whether it is true or false. The innocent party may claim damages under the tort of deceit and/or rescind the contract.

Negligent misrepresentation

This is an untrue statement which is believed to be true but there are no grounds for believing it to be so. There are two types of negligent misrepresentation – under common law and under the Misrepresentation Act 1967. The remedy is damages and/or rescission.

Innocent misrepresentation

This is an untrue statement which the maker believes to be true and has grounds for believing it to be so. The normal remedy is rescission, although under the Misrepresentation Act 1967 the court may award damages instead.

DURESS

> **Crucial concept**   **Duress.** Under the common law a contract was voidable if a party entered into it as a result of actual or threatened physical violence. More recently, the doctrine of economic duress has developed under which one party takes advantage of the other to negotiate or rene-gotiate terms of the contract in their favour.

Factors that the court will take into account are whether the claimant has any choice in complying with the other party's terms and whether there was a threat to carry out an unlawful act.

> **Crucial tip**   It is sometimes difficult to differentiate between hard bargaining and economic duress.

> Crucial concept　**Undue influence** is improper pressure put on one party by the other to make them enter into a contract, for example to get them to leave money or a house in a will. It can render the contract voidable.

If there is a fiduciary relationship between the parties, for example between parent and child or doctor and patient, it is presumed that there has been undue influence and it is up to the party who benefits from the contract to rebut this presumption.

　If there is no fiduciary relationship then it is up to the party who is claiming undue influence to prove it.

Quick test

1. What is a misrepresentation?
2. What is meant by unilateral mistake?

Section 4　　How contracts come to an end

What are you studying?

This section describes the ways in which a contract may come to an end or be discharged. It also describes the remedies available to the innocent party if the contract ends due to a breach by the other party.

How will you be assessed on this?

You will need to know how a contract may come to an end and the remedies for breach of contract. Questions may ask a student to identify if there is a breach of contract and if so what remedy would be available to the innocent party.

　A contract may come to an end in one of the following ways:

- performance;
- agreement;
- frustration;
- breach.

Performance

> Crucial concept　**Performance.** If both parties have carried out their obligations, the contract comes to an end. The parties must have carried out exactly what they agreed to do.

Example: Cutter v Powell (1795)

Cutter was employed by Powell as part of the crew on a ship sailing from Jamaica to London. He was to receive 30 guineas when the ship reached Liverpool. He died 19 days before the ship's arrival. His widow was not entitled to any of his pay as he had not performed all his obligations under the contract.

Entire and divisible contracts

If a contract is an entire contract then payment will not be due until the whole of the contract has been performed. The contract in *Cutter* v *Powell* was an entire contract. Contracts may also be divisible which means that payments may be made at various stages throughout the term of the contract. It is usual for a contract of employment to be a divisible contract, where the employee gets paid at weekly or monthly intervals.

Substantial performance

If the majority of the contract has been completed then payment must be made, although a small deduction may be made for work not completed.

Example: Hoenig v *Issacs* (1952)

The claimant carried out decorating and furnishing to the defendant's flat. Some minor work remained uncompleted. The defendant was obliged to pay the agreed price of £750 less a sum of £56, which was the sum needed to remedy the uncompleted work.

How you decide if a contract has been substantially performed would be by reference to what was agreed to be done and what was left undone. Usually, if the work has only been partially performed in such a way as to provide the claimant with no actual benefit, it is unlikely to be substantial performance. For example, if a builder puts on half a roof this is unlikely to be substantial performance.

Agreement

> Crucial concept   **Agreement.** The parties may agree to bring the contract to an end. There may be a clause in the contract as to how this may happen, for example in a contract of employment. If there is no such clause, then the parties must have another agreement to end the contract and they must provide consideration.

If neither party has performed his obligations then the consideration would be the promise by each party to end the contract. If only one party has performed his obligations then there must be some other consideration by the other party to release him from his obligations.

Frustration

> Crucial concept   **Frustration.** A contract will be frustrated if after it has been formed but before it as been performed, something occurs which makes performance impossible.

Frustration may occur under the following circumstances:

- the subject matter no longer exists;

- one of the parties becomes ill or dies;

- the event on which the contract is based fails to take place;

- changes in the law make the contract illegal;

- government interference.

The subject matter no longer exists

If the subject matter of the contract is destroyed after formation but before performance of the contract, the contract will be frustrated.

Example: Taylor v Caldwell (1863)
The claimant had a contract to hire a music hall for a series of concerts. The hall was destroyed by fire before any of the contracts could take place. It was held that the contract was frustrated.

One of the parties becomes ill or dies

If the performance of the contract depends upon one person, death will frustrate it and illness will if it has a sufficiently serious effect upon performance.

Example: Condor v Barron Knights (1966)
A drummer in a band became ill and was only able to perform for four nights a week out of an expected seven on a long term contract. It was held that the contract was frustrated.

The event on which the contract is based fails to take place

Example: Krell v Henry (1903)
The claimant hired a room to overlook the Coronation procession of Edward VII. The event did not take place because the King was ill. The contract was frustrated.

Changes in the law make the contract illegal

This may occur, for example, if a party has a contract with an overseas country and war is declared upon that country. The contract would then become illegal as you cannot trade with the enemy in times of war.

Government interference

A contract may be frustrated if there is intervention by the government or a government agency. For example, a contract of employment will be frustrated if the employee is sent to prison.

A contract will not be frustrated if it becomes more difficult or more costly to perform.

Example: Tsakiroglou v Noblee & Thorl (1961)
A contract to deliver goods from Port Sudan to Hamburg was not frustrated when the Suez Canal closed even though delivery would take longer and be more expensive.

Breach and remedies for breach of contract

Crucial concept | **Breach.** If a condition of the contract is breached, in addition to claiming damages the innocent party may bring the contract to an end.

Crucial concept | The main **remedies for breach of contract** are:
- damages;
- specific performance;
- injunction.

DAMAGES

The most common remedy for the injured party is financial compensation in the form of damages. The parties may insert a clause into the contract, which states the amount to which damages will be limited in the event of a breach. Damages agreed in advance are known as *liquidated damages*. Damages which are not agreed in advance are known as *unliquidated damages* and the amount awarded is intended to compensate the claimant for his loss.

Liquidated damages and penalty clauses

The courts will usually recognise a liquidated damages clause if it is a genuine pre-estimate of the loss. Any clause intended to penalise a party where the amount payable in the event of a breach is far in excess of the actual loss will be ignored by the courts.

> Crucial tip   Building contracts insert liquidated damages clauses to overcome problems of weather and overrun periods.

Remoteness of damage

When considering whether damages should be awarded, the court will consider the rule in *Hadley v Baxendale* (1854) which states that damages will only be awarded for losses which arise naturally and are in the contemplation of the parties in the event of a breach at the time the contract was made.

Example: Victoria Laundry v Newman Industries (1949)
The claimants ordered a boiler which they asked to be delivered in June. It arrived in November. As a result the claimant lost a number of lucrative contracts. The defendants were liable for the normal losses of profit between June and November but not for the loss of the lucrative contracts as they were unaware of these.

SPECIFIC PERFORMANCE

If the court considers that damages are not an adequate remedy. It may order a party who is in breach to perform his obligations under the contract. For example, to continue with the sale of a property.

INJUNCTION

An injunction is an order by the court which orders a person to do or not to do a certain act.

Example: Warner Bros v Nelson (1937)
An actress agreed to work only for Warner Bros. When she entered into a contract with another party, Warner Bros were awarded an injunction to prevent her from doing so.

> Crucial tip   Specific performance and injunction are equitable remedies awarded at the court's discretion.

Quick test

1. Explain the difference between liquidated and unliquidated damages.
2. When will a contract be frustrated?

Crucial examples

1. (a) What elements must a legally binding contract contain?
   (b) Describe the effects of the postal rule.

2. (a) Explain the difference between express and implied terms.
   (b) Explain the difference between conditions, warranties and innominate terms.

3. What factors may make a contract voidable?

4. (a) In what ways may a contract come to an end?
   (b) What remedies are available to the innocent party when there has been a breach of contract?

Answers

1. (a) A legally binding contract must contain:

   - an offer;
   - acceptance;
   - consideration;
   - a legal purpose;
   - intention to be legally bound; and
   - capacity.

   (b) Where acceptance is by letter it is valid as soon as it is posted if it is addressed correctly.

2. (a) Express terms are terms which are agreed between the parties to the contract. Implied terms have not been agreed between the parties but are implied into the contract by statute, common law or custom.

   (b) A condition is a major term of a contract. If it is broken the contract may be brought to an end and damages claimed. A warranty is a minor term of the contract. If it is broken only damages may be claimed. An innominate term is one where it is not possible to tell whether it is a condition or warranty until after the breach has occurred.

3. These are mistake, misrepresentation, duress and undue influence. They are explained in more detail in Section 3.

4. (a) A contract may come to an end by performance, agreement, frustration or breach.

   (b) The main remedies for breach of contract are damages, specific performance and injunction.
   See Section 4 for further details.

Crucial reading and research

Upex, *Davies on Contract,* 8th edn., Sweet & Maxwell.
MacIntyre, *Business Law,* Longman, Chapters 3 to 7.
Keenan and Riches, *Business Law,* 6th edn., Longman, Chapters 7 to 9.

CHAPTER 3

SALE AND SUPPLY OF
GOODS AND SERVICES

Chapter summary

This chapter provides details of the legal rights and duties concerning the sale and purchase of goods. It also deals with the acquisition of goods and services and shows how the legal framework regulates such transactions.

Studying this chapter will help you to:

- understand and use the appropriate legal terms to describe a sale of goods transaction or a supply of goods and services transaction;

- identify the statutory rights given to buyers under the implied terms of the Sale of Goods Act 1979 (as amended) or the Supply of Goods and Services Act 1982 (as amended);

- recognise the legal requirements necessary to transfer goods from seller to buyer and the consequences of a failure to observe those requirements;

- be aware of the seller and buyer's rights and duties in the event of a breach of contract;

- distinguish contracts for the sale of goods from those that deal with the sale/supply of goods and services.

Assessment targets

Target 1: identifying the difference between the sale of goods and the supply of goods and services

You will have to be familiar with the types of transactions that are classed as sale of goods transactions and those which are classed as supply of goods and services. Exercise 1 at the end of this chapter will test whether you can recognise which Act applies in each case.

Target 2: identifying the implied terms in the Sale of Goods Act

You will have to recognise whether there is evidence of any breach of the implied terms and what the buyer's remedies may be. Exercise 2 at the end of this chapter tests your ability to decide if there are any breaches and if so what are the buyer's rights.

Target 3: distinguishing between specific and unascertained goods and consider who bears the risk for such goods

You will have to know the difference between these two types of goods and identify where risk lies. Exercise 3 at the end of this chapter will test your ability to differentiate between specific and unascertained goods and attribute risk.

Target 4: understanding contractual rules as to delivery and payment for goods

You must consider the buyer's rights where goods are delivered incorrectly. Exercise 4 at the end of this chapter will test your knowledge of the buyer's rights in this situation.

Crucial terms, cases and Acts

Sale of goods contract

Section 12 (implied condition as to title)

Section 13 (implied condition as to description)

Section 14 (implied conditions as to satisfactory quality and fitness for purpose)

Rogers v *Parish (Scarborough) Ltd* (1987)

The difference between satisfactory quality and fitness for purpose

Section 15 (implied condition as to sale by sample)

Specific goods

Unascertained goods

Transfer of property and risk

Tarling v *Baxter* (1827)

Reservation of title by the seller

Exceptions to the rule that you cannot give what you do not own

Delivery and acceptance of goods

Buyer's acceptance

Seller's remedies

Buyer's remedies

Implied terms as to the supply of goods

Goods supplied for hire

Implied terms as to the supply of services

Relevant links

Refer to **Chapter 2** for basic contractual rights and duties and especially section 2 for unfair contract terms.

Refer to **Chapter 4** where a person is not a party to a contract and suffers damage/ injury through the use of defective goods or services. Their civil remedy may lie in the tort of negligence or under the Consumer Protection Act 1987.

Section I   What is classified as a sale of goods?

What are you studying?

In this section we identify what would be classed as a sale of goods for the purposes of the Sale of Goods Act 1979 (as amended). This means identifying what is a sale, what are classed as goods and when the purchaser actually acquires them.

How will you be assessed on this?

It is unlikely that you would have to deal with a question that simply required you to say whether a contract was a sale of goods contract. It is far more likely that you would need to be able to work out whether it was a contract falling under the 1979 Act in order to be able to go on and consider whether any other Sale of Goods Act rules applied to the problem.

Sale of goods contract

> Crucial concept   A contract for the sale of goods is a contract by which the seller transfers or agrees to transfer the property in the goods to the buyer for a money consideration called the price.

There are a number of ways that people acquire goods. They do not always buy them under a sale of goods transaction. If they are not bought in accordance with the definition as set out in the Sale of Goods Act 1979, then it will not be classed as a sale under the Act. The Act only deals with buyers' and sellers' contractual duties and remedies.

For a transaction to be subject to the Sale of Goods Act 1979 it must meet certain criteria:

- *It must be a sale not a gift or bailment.* This means that if someone else buys the goods and gives them to you as a present, you are not a purchaser according to the terms of the Act. Bailment occurs where you are given possession of goods to take care of them for someone else and are expected to return them to that person upon their request or at the end of an agreed period.

- *There must be a money consideration or price paid for the goods.* If you merely exchange one item for another this would not be a sale of goods but a straight swap. If you part exchange goods this can be a sale of goods transaction because you are making up part of the price with money.

- *The item you buy must be classed as goods as defined by the Act.* These can usually be defined as personal goods of a moveable type, for example a car or a CD player, the kind of goods you would buy in a high street shop. For the purposes of the Act, land (or things you cannot remove from the land) buildings, cheques or money (currency) are not goods.

- *There must be a buyer and a seller capable of entering into a contract.*

- *There has to be a transfer of the property in the goods.* In this context 'property' means a transfer of ownership from seller to buyer. This means that simply gaining possession of goods does not mean that you have acquired the goods according to this Act. Therefore hiring or leasing goods is not a sale of goods transaction nor is it a sale of goods transaction if you acquire the goods under a hire-purchase agreement.

> Crucial tip
>
> Do not confuse a hire-purchase agreement with a hire agreement. In a hire-purchase agreement the aim is for the hirer to finally acquire ownership of the goods whereas in a hire agreement the hirer is only acquiring a right to possess the goods for so long as the agreement lasts. Do not confuse either of these with a straightforward sale of goods transaction.

Quick test

1. What is a sale of goods?
2. Define the terms 'goods', 'property' and 'price' in the context of the Sale of Goods Act 1979.

Section 2	Terms implied by the Sale of Goods Act 1979

What are you studying?

Some terms in a sale of goods contract are classed as implied terms. You need to know what these terms are as some cannot be excluded in any contract and others cannot be excluded when the seller sells in the course of a business and the buyer is a consumer.

How will you be assessed on this?

This is an area of law that often features in sale of goods questions. A question may deal almost exclusively with a buyer's rights under the implied terms. It is important to know what each of the sections of the Act deal with. You should be able to recognise whether there has been a breach of any of these terms and the buyer's rights where a breach occurs.

The Sale of Goods Act 1979 provides implied terms which protect the buyer. These terms are vital to consumers as they offer the buyer specific rights which cannot be taken away by a business seller (see Chapter 2, section 2 Unfair Contract Terms Act 1977). If these terms are broken they are treated as conditions in the contract and would entitle the buyer to rescind the contract.

Title

> Crucial concept
>
> **Section 12 (implied condition as to title).** There is an assumption that the seller has the right to sell the goods and once he has sold the goods to the buyer he undertakes that the buyer's title will not be questioned or interfered with.

This contractual right applies to all sales of goods transactions, whether private or business sales. Breach of this term would entitle the buyer to obtain a full refund on the price.

> Crucial tip
>
> Someone who merely transfers possession or use of goods is not necessarily transferring ownership. It is vital that the buyer is satisfied that he has acquired full title to the goods.

Description

> **Crucial concept**
>
> **Section 13 (implied condition as to description).** Under s. 13 there is an implied condition that goods must correspond with their description. Goods are sold by description when a buyer relies on the description never having seen the goods, for example when buying by mail order.

Even goods that are seen and selected by the buyer from the seller's stock can still be goods sold by description, for example in a self-service store. The buyer would rely on the description printed on the packaging, for example 500 gms milk chocolate. Usually it is implied that the buyer is relying upon the seller's description of the goods but if the buyer indicates that he is not relying upon the seller's description, he cannot claim a breach of this term if the goods do not turn out to be what he expected.

This contractual right applies to all sales of goods transactions, whether private or business sales.

> **Crucial tip**
>
> If the goods turn out to be defective as to quality or condition it does not mean that they fail to match their description. For example, a box of chocolates described as soft-centred milk chocolates and 250 gms in weight are not in breach of description if they turn out to be mouldy. That is an issue of quality not description.

Satisfactory quality and fitness for purpose

> **Crucial concept**
>
> **Section 14 (implied conditions as to satisfactory quality and fitness for purpose).** Goods must be of satisfactory quality (s. 14(2)) and fit for the purpose (s. 14(3)) for which they have been sold.

> **Crucial tip**
>
> Conditions as to quality and fitness only apply to business sales not private sales.

Section 14(1) sets out the basic principle that where goods are purchased, it is the buyer's responsibility to ensure that the goods are of the quality he requires. The rule of *caveat emptor* (let the buyer beware) applies, and the seller is not liable for the defective goods.

However, under (s. 14(2)) of the Act if goods are sold *in the course of a business* a condition will be implied into the contract of sale that the goods will be of satisfactory quality.

Sales in the course of a business are interpreted very widely and, for example, even a fisherman selling his old vessel is said to be selling it in the course of a business even though he does not normally deal in the business of selling trawlers. See *Stevenson v Rogers* (1999).

SATISFACTORY QUALITY

Goods are of a satisfactory quality if they meet the standard that a reasonable person would regard as satisfactory taking into account description, price (if relevant) and all other relevant circumstances.

The quality of goods is judged (but not necessarily exclusively) by:

- fitness for all purposes for which goods of the kind in question are commonly supplied;

- appearance and finish;

- freedom from minor defects;

- safety;

- durability.

Crucial case	***Rogers v Parish (Scarborough) Ltd (1987).*** A new £16,000 Range Rover with defective oil seals, gearbox problems and poor bodywork, despite still being capable of being driven, was not of satisfactory quality. In this case the court considered the finish and appearance of the vehicle and also concluded that 'quality' vehicles should be free from minor defects.

Crucial tip	Second-hand goods are still expected to be of satisfactory quality but defects may appear more quickly than they would in a new item.

There is no implied condition as to satisfactory quality when defects are specifically brought to the buyer's attention by the seller before purchase or in respect of defects which the buyer ought to have noticed if he had examined the goods. For example, if goods are labelled as water damaged, a buyer cannot later complain of unsatisfactory quality when he notices water stains.

Crucial tip	The buyer is not under an obligation to examine the goods.

A seller's responsibility for the satisfactory quality of goods can extend to the containers goods are supplied in and their user instructions. For example, goods could be unsatisfactory if the glass bottles they came in exploded or the warning/user instructions were faulty.

Where a consignment of goods turns out to be partly defective, no matter how trivial the defect, they may still be rejected by a consumer. However, where the buyer is another business and the defect is minor, the buyer cannot reject the goods although he could sue for loss.

FITNESS FOR PURPOSE

Where a business seller sells goods and the buyer expressly or by implication makes known to the seller any particular purpose for which the goods are being bought, there is an implied condition that the goods are reasonably fit for that purpose; unless circumstances show that the buyer did not rely, or it was unreasonable for him to have relied, on the skill or judgement of the seller.

If the buyer's purpose for the goods is obvious, he need not expressly state his purpose. For example, a hot water bottle has one obvious purpose and if it is not fit for that purpose because it bursts scalding the user when filled with very hot water, it fails the fitness test.

The buyer must show that he relied on the seller's skill and judgement. If the buyer indicates to the seller that he has greater expertise or ignores the seller's advice as to a suitable product for his use, there will not be an implied term as to fitness for purpose.

Whether goods are fit for the purpose is a question of fact. The age, condition and price paid for the goods will be taken into account.

Even trivial or latent defects can render goods unfit. Therefore a seller may sell defective goods and be unaware of the defect but still be liable. For example, if a milkman sells milk with typhoid germs in it he is liable even though he is unaware of the condition of the milk. The buyer relied on him to sell germ free milk.

> **Crucial tip**
>
> The initial responsibility for defective goods rests with the seller rather than the manufacturer so it is not the buyer's responsibility to complain to the manufacturer.

> **Crucial concept**
>
> **The difference between satisfactory quality and fitness for purpose.** Goods which are not of satisfactory quality have a manufacturing defect which the perfect article would not have had. In other words, it is the right article for the buyer but it is faulty. Whereas an article not fit for its purpose can be a perfectly manufactured article and of satisfactory quality but unfit for the buyer's use. For example, if a seller advises the buyer to purchase a certain make of printer for use with his computer and the printer is incompatible with the computer despite the buyer having told the seller what make it is, the printer may be a 'perfect' printer but the wrong printer for the buyer's needs.

Sale by sample

> **Crucial concept**
>
> **Section 15 (implied condition as to sale by sample).** A contract of sale is a contract for sale by sample where there is an express or implied term to that effect in the contract. Just because there is a sample provided does not make a contract of sale by sample. There must be evidence that the parties intended it to be a sale by sample.

The bulk of the goods must correspond in quality with the sample and the buyer must have a reasonable opportunity of comparing the bulk with the sample. The bulk of the goods must be free of defects which would cause them to be of unsatisfactory quality and which would not be revealed upon a reasonable examination of the sample. However, it would be assumed that a buyer would examine the sample, and if defects ought to have been spotted in the sample the buyer cannot reject the bulk if the same defect appears in the bulk goods.

> **Crucial tip**
>
> Manufacturers' guarantees usually consist of undertakings by manufacturers to repair or replace faulty goods, within a specified time. A manufacturer's guarantee cannot replace or deny a consumer their statutory rights. It is given in addition to statutory rights.

Quick test

1. How would you judge whether goods were of satisfactory quality?
2. What is the difference between satisfactory quality and fitness for purpose?
3. What is the consumer's usual remedy for a breach of an implied term?

Section 3 — Transfer of property in the goods

What are you studying?

Transfer of goods, which in the context of the Sale of Goods Act 1979 means acquiring ownership of the goods, is vitally important as certain obligations such as taking on the risk for the goods usually passes to the buyer when the property in the goods is transferred. The remedies that are available to the seller if the buyer fails to pay will be different according to whether the ownership in the goods has been transferred.

How will you be assessed on this?

For examination purposes you should be able to distinguish between specific goods and unascertained goods. Questions that deal with transfer of property will require you to know whether goods are specific or unascertained. A problem question may require you to identify who will bear the risk if goods are destroyed. It is also useful for you to understand the concept of reservation of title and the effects it may have upon a buyer's ownership of goods.

The 1979 Act lays down rules as to when the property in the goods is transferred and classifies goods into two categories known as specific goods and unascertained goods. Depending upon whether the goods are classed as specific or unascertained will determine when the property in the goods passes.

Specific goods

> **Crucial concept**
>
> **Specific goods.** The property in the goods passes at the time the contract is made provided the goods are identified and agreed upon at the time of the contract, and are in a deliverable state. This can mean that the goods have not been delivered to the buyer or paid for but are technically owned by the buyer. The property in specific goods can pass according to the terms agreed upon by the contracting parties but in the absence of any special arrangements the above rule will prevail.

If the seller has to do something to the goods such as weigh them or label them, they do not become specific goods in a deliverable state until that task is performed and the buyer knows the goods are ready. For example, if the contract calls for the seller to fit a CD player into the buyer's new car, the car is not in a deliverable state until the CD player is fitted and the seller notifies the buyer it is ready. Where the buyer takes goods on sale or return, the property in them does not pass until the buyer indicates to the seller that he has accepted them.

Unascertained goods

> **Crucial concept**
>
> **Unascertained goods.** The property in the goods does not pass until the goods have been ascertained. This means that deliverable goods must be unconditionally appropriated to the buyer's contract with the consent of buyer and seller.

For example, if a seller has ten identical mountain bikes and the buyer agrees to buy one, the goods will not become ascertained until one specific bike is set aside and labelled for that buyer.

Goods which have to be manufactured or acquired by the seller are known as *future* goods and are usually treated as unascertained goods.

Where the buyer's goods are part of a larger consignment, they cannot be ascertained until the rest of the goods have been disposed of. For example, if the buyer orders 20 cameras from a consignment of 50, when the seller has disposed of 30 cameras the remaining 20 belong to the buyer. This is known as *ascertainment by exhaustion*.

Problems could arise where the buyer has paid in advance for goods which are still unascertained because they are part of a larger bulk consignment and the seller becomes insolvent. The buyer cannot point to the precise part of the consignment which is his. The buyer is treated as co-owner of the goods and so would not be treated as an unsecured creditor in the event of the seller's insolvency.

Transfer of property and risk

Crucial concept	**Transfer of property and risk.** Risk passes with the transfer of property so once the buyer has the property in the goods he has the risk. This means that even if the buyer has not taken possession of the goods he may still have the risk.

Crucial case	*Tarling v Baxter* (1827). A haystack was sold to a buyer who did not take immediate delivery of it. The haystack burnt down. It was held that the buyer still had to pay the seller the full price as the risk passed to the buyer when he made the contract and it was immaterial that it burnt down before he had removed it.

Crucial tip	It is vital that the buyer insures the goods from the moment the property in the goods passes to him even if they are still with the seller or in transit as if they are lost or damaged at that time he will bear the cost.

Crucial concept	**Reservation of title by seller.** The seller may stipulate in the contract that he intends to retain ownership of the goods until some condition is fulfilled, even if the buyer is given possession of the goods. Usually the condition is that the buyer has to pay for the goods before title will pass.

This is often known as a 'Romalpa' clause (taken from the name of a leading case on the subject) and is used by a seller to protect himself if the buyer becomes insolvent. As the buyer does not own the goods the seller can reclaim them and does not have to make a claim as an unsecured trade creditor in the buyer's insolvency. Unless this type of clause is very carefully drafted it may not give the seller any protection where the buyer has resold the goods or the goods have been used in a manufacturing process and cannot be reclaimed in their original state.

Quick test

1. What is the difference between specific and unascertained goods?
2. When does risk usually pass?
3. Why do sellers impose reservation of title clauses in sale of goods contracts?

| Section 4 | Sale by a person who is not the owner |

What are you studying?

A buyer cannot acquire a better title to goods than the seller has. Therefore it is generally accepted that an innocent third party who acquires goods from someone who does not have authority to pass on a good title will find themselves having to return the goods to the true owner. There are exceptions to this rule and these will be examined in this section.

How will you be assessed on this?

An examination question may feature a problem where goods have come into the possession of an innocent buyer who is unaware of the history and ownership of the goods. You may be required to work out whether the original owner can claim the goods or whether they will remain in the possession of the innocent buyer. You will need to know that a seller with defective title cannot pass on good title to his buyer unless one of the exceptions listed below apply.

| Crucial tip | The innocent purchaser could sue the seller for breach of s. 12(1) of the Sale of Goods Act 1979 but often a seller who has attempted to sell goods which he does not own will have disappeared before the innocent buyer realises he has not got a good title to the goods. |

Exceptions to the rule that you cannot give what you do not own

| Crucial concept | **Exceptions to the rule that you cannot give what you do not own.** The exceptions are:
● estoppel;
● agency;
● special powers of sale;
● sale under a voidable title;
● sale by seller in possession;
● sale by buyer in possession. |

ESTOPPEL

If the true owner by his conduct allows the innocent buyer to believe that the seller has authority to sell the goods, the buyer will acquire good title to them. However, just because the true owner is negligent and loses his goods does not mean that the finder can justifiably sell them to an innocent buyer. For estoppel to operate the true owner must have represented in some way that the seller could sell his goods.

AGENCY

An owner, known as the 'principal', who appoints another person known as an 'agent' to sell his goods on his behalf cannot deny an innocent buyer good title to the goods if the agent has sold them in accordance with the principal's instructions. The buyer may acquire good title to the goods even if the agent has exceeded his principal's instructions.

The buyer may assume that the agent has the usual authority that goes with his job or make a claim where the owner has allowed the buyer to believe that the agent has greater authority than he actually has. Where an agent is classed as a mercantile agent (or factor) the innocent buyer may have an even stronger claim to the goods.

SPECIAL POWERS OF SALE

A pawnbroker has power to sell goods which have been pledged to him if the loan is not repaid.

A court can also order the sale of goods which are the subject of legal proceedings if it deems it necessary or desirable.

SALE UNDER A VOIDABLE TITLE

Where a buyer, who has obtained his title by fraud, sells the goods on to an innocent buyer who buys in good faith, the innocent buyer will acquire good title to the goods if the original owner does not avoid the contract with the fraudulent buyer before the resale.

The original owner can avoid the contract by notifying the fraudulent buyer or taking some other step, such as informing the police.

> **Crucial tip** Owners who accept cheques from buyers and release the goods to them before clearing the cheque may find themselves losing their goods to an innocent third party who buys them from the fraudster.

SALE BY SELLER IN POSSESSION

Where the goods remain in the seller's possession even after sale and the seller resells the goods to a second buyer, who buys in good faith and without notice of the first sale, the second buyer acquires good title to the goods. The first buyer would have to sue the seller for breach of contract.

SALE BY A BUYER IN POSSESSION

Where the buyer takes possession of the goods with the seller's consent but the seller has retained title to the goods, an innocent third party who buys the goods from the buyer in good faith and without notice of the seller's claim to them acquires a good title to the goods.

This provision does not apply to persons who act as buyers but who only have possession of goods under a hire-purchase agreement. They are hirers not buyers. If a *bona fide* private purchaser of a motor vehicle which is still the subject of a hire-purchase agreement buys in good faith without knowledge of the hire-purchase agreement then he acquires good title.

> **Crucial tip** This exception does not operate to protect an innocent buyer who buys through a chain of sellers where the original seller was a thief.

Quick test

1. What are the exceptions to the rule that a buyer cannot assume a better title to goods than that of the seller?
2. Why should you not release goods to a buyer before his cheque has been cleared?

Buyer's and seller's rights under a sale of goods contract

What are you studying?

This section examines the seller's duty to deliver the goods to the buyer in accordance with the contract terms and the buyer's duty to accept the goods and pay for them.

How will you be assessed?

A question may feature a problem concerning payment and delivery of goods. It is necessary to know what may happen if the goods are not delivered as agreed under the contract or what the consequences would be if the buyer refused to accept delivery or pay for the goods as agreed. You should also be aware of the rights and remedies a party may have if the contract is not performed correctly.

Delivery and acceptance

Crucial concept	**Delivery and acceptance of goods.** The seller has a duty to deliver the goods and the buyer has a duty to accept them.
	The seller should deliver the goods at the agreed time and place and by the agreed method. This could mean allowing the buyer to collect them if that is the agreed method. If a specific time for delivery is agreed, the seller will be in breach of contract if he fails to deliver at the specified time. If no time is specified, delivery must be within a reasonable time.

Crucial tip	Remember to check who will bear the risk if the goods are to be delivered by a carrier.

If the seller delivers a larger quantity of goods, the buyer can accept what is delivered and pay for them or simply reject the excess. If the seller delivers less than agreed, the buyer can accept what is delivered and pay for it at the contract rate. In either case the buyer can reject the whole if he chooses. If the buyer is not a consumer, delivery of slightly less or more of the goods will not entitle the buyer to reject the consignment.

Where goods are defective or do not conform to the contract, the buyer can reject all or part of the consignment. For example, if the buyer ordered 250 carpet tiles and 25 were water damaged he could keep the 225 undamaged carpet tiles and reject the damaged ones or he could keep the 225 undamaged carpet tiles and some of the 25 damaged ones if he could use them in places where the damage wouldn't be seen or he could reject the whole 250.

If the goods are to be delivered in instalments, the seller should deliver the correct quantity and quality of goods in each instalment and the buyer should accept each correctly delivered instalment. If a breach occurs, the ratio of the breach to the contract as a whole and the likelihood of it being repeated will determine whether the entire contract can be repudiated.

Crucial tip	Unless the buyer has agreed to accept delivery by instalments he is not bound to do so.

> **Crucial concept** **Buyer's acceptance.** The buyer is bound to accept the goods the seller delivers if they are in accordance with the contract.

The buyer has accepted the goods when he:

- indicates to the seller he has accepted the goods;
- resells the goods;
- does acts inconsistent with the seller's ownership, for example modifies them or keeps them for an unreasonably long time without indicating he has rejected them.

A consumer does not lose the right to reject the goods until he has had an opportunity to examine them. This usually means a reasonable opportunity to use the goods not just having them in his possession. If the buyer continues to use goods which he knows are faulty he will lose his right to reject them.

> **Crucial tip** The buyer does not accept the goods merely because he signed a delivery note or requested or agreed to a repair being carried out.

The buyer will be in breach of contract if he fails to take delivery of goods at the agreed time and pay for them at the agreed time. Delivery and payment usually go together.

> **Crucial tip** Failing to pay on time is usually a breach of warranty not a breach of condition.

Remedies

> **Crucial concept** **Seller's remedies.** The seller has two remedies against the buyer:
> - where the buyer has not paid for the goods the seller can sue for the price;
> - where the buyer has wrongfully refused to accept the goods he can sue for damages.

> **Crucial concept** **Buyer's remedies.** Where the seller breaks the contract the buyer can reject the goods and/or sue for damages. The buyer will usually be entitled to repudiate the contract where a condition has been broken (see the implied term, ss. 12–15 of the Sale of Goods Act 1979). In other instances such as a breach of warranty or non delivery he may sue the seller for damages.

The seller may also have remedies against the goods such as stopping them in transit or reselling them to a second buyer.

Quick test

1. What rights does a buyer have if:
   (a) the seller does not deliver the right quantity of goods;
   (b) the seller does not deliver goods of a satisfactory quality?
2. Under what circumstances may a buyer be said to have accepted goods delivered by the seller?

Section 6 — Supply of goods and services

What are you studying?

A buyer is protected under the Sale of Goods Act 1979 where goods are purchased for a monetary consideration. The 1979 Act does not cover goods obtained by other means, for example hire, barter or goods supplied in conjunction with services. The Supply of Goods and Services Act 1982 gives statutory protection to buyers acquiring goods along with a service as well as some protection for those provided with poor services.

How will you be assessed?

It is possible that you would have to decide whether a contract is a sale of goods contract or a supply of goods and services transaction. It is important to know what types of transactions come under the Supply of Goods and Services Act 1982, for example hire, exchange, rental, leasing, supply of services (with or without goods/materials supplied). You should familiarise yourself with the differing provisions that govern supply of goods and services.

If the contract is for work or services *and* goods or materials, for example a contract for servicing a car where parts are supplied, the supply of the goods is covered by Part I of the Supply of Goods and Services Act 1982. The work or services element of the job is covered by Part II of the Act.

> **Crucial concept** — **Implied terms as to the supply of goods.** Where goods are supplied in conjunction with services and the buyer will acquire ownership of the goods there are implied conditions as to title, description, quality, fitness and sample.

Implied terms as to the supply of goods
SECTION 2 – (TITLE)

Section 2 assumes the supplier has the right to transfer the property in the goods to the customer. This provision cannot be excluded in a contract.

SECTION 3 – (DESCRIPTION)

Goods supplied will correspond with their description.

> **Crucial tip** — In some goods and services contracts the goods or materials used cannot be specified until the contract is underway. For example, supplying parts when servicing a car.

SECTION 4 – (SATISFACTORY QUALITY AND FITNESS)

These provisions are similar to those contained within the Sale of Goods Act 1979.

SECTION 5 – (SAMPLE)

This provision is similar to that contained within the Sale of Goods Act 1979.

> **Crucial concept** — **Goods supplied for hire.** Where goods are supplied under a hire contract the implied terms match so far as possible the implied terms under the Sale of Goods Act (ss. 12–15).
>
> Sections 7–10 apply to commercial/consumer contracts of hire.

> Crucial tip — These provisions do not apply to hire-purchase agreements.

> Crucial tip — Sections 3–5 and 8–10 cannot be excluded/restricted where the buyer is a consumer and the terms are subject to a test of reasonableness in a business to business transaction. (See Chapter 2: section 2 Unfair Contract Terms Act 1977.)

Implied terms as to the supply of services

> Crucial tip — **Implied terms as to the supply of services.** Where services are supplied (with or without goods) there are implied terms as to the quality of service, the time it takes to complete the service and the cost.

The services supplied in the course of a business must be:

- *Section 13 (carried out with reasonable care and skill)*. This is usually seen as the ordinary skill of an ordinary competent person in that trade or profession, for example the competent accountant, the competent plumber.

- *Section 14 (carried out within a reasonable time)*. This applies where a time has not been specified in the contract.

- *Section 15 (carried out for a reasonable charge)*. This applies where a charge/fee has not been agreed at the time of the contract. If no charge is agreed at the outset of the contract or there is no calculable scale, it is a question of fact as to what is reasonable.

A breach of these implied terms will usually result in damages but may result in repudiation of the contract if the breach is serious.

If there is no contractual relationship between the supplier of the goods or services and the ultimate consumer, then in an action for damage or injury caused by the suppliers, fault may be based in the tort of negligence or the Consumer Protection Act 1987. (See Chapter 4 on tort.)

Quick test

1. What types of transactions are covered under the Supply of Goods and Services Act 1982?
2. Which section of the 1982 Act applies if goods supplied together with a service turn out to be unsatisfactory?
3. Which section of the 1982 Act applies if the workmanship/services supplied turn out to be unsatisfactory?

Crucial examples

1. In the following situations state whether the transaction would fall under the Sale of Goods Act 1979, the Supply of Goods and Services Act 1982 or neither of these.
   (a) Amanda takes her car to a garage for its 30,000 mile service. The garage carries out the service and charges her £132 labour costs and £78 for a new battery, wiper blades and oil.

(b) Clive goes to a computer sales centre and agrees to buy the Pineapple mark II PC from them if they will take his Pineapple mark I in part exchange.

(c) Farinda purchases a three piece suite from ABC Furniture Stores on hire purchase terms.

(d) George rents a video machine from his local TV store.

(e) Edwin goes into a gallery and sees a selection of paintings by 'Fleet' (a popular new artist). He buys one of Fleet's paintings after looking at a selection.

If Edwin had been so impressed by Fleet's work that he had commissioned a work from him would it have made any difference to your answer?

2. Anne bought a new washing machine from an electrical store two weeks ago. Can Anne reject the machine and on what grounds if:

(a) It is scratched but works perfectly well.

(b) It does not work but can be fixed easily.

(c) She bought it with a dent on the casing which had been pointed out to her by the seller before she bought it.

(d) The first time Anne used the machine it made terrible grinding noises. She had not used it during the first two weeks she owned it. Upon complaining to the seller he said he would come out and try to repair it for her but would not refund the purchase price to her as she had had the machine too long to expect a total refund.

3. Donald ordered a new 'Supergreen' ride-on lawnmower from Sureways Garden Supplies Ltd. He asked the seller to fit special tyres to the machine before he took delivery of it. Sureways premises were ram-raided the evening before Donald was due to take delivery of his lawnmower. The lawnmower was damaged in the raid before the seller was able to do the final pre-delivery check but after the new tyres had been fitted.

Who will have to bear the cost of the damage to the lawnmower – Donald or Sureways?

4. Sue ordered 12 bags of mushroom compost for her garden from a local mushroom farm for £18. The seller turned up at Sue's with 20 bags and asked Sue to pay £30. She told the delivery man that she had only ordered 12 bags but he said he had been told to deliver all the bags on the lorry and as she was the last delivery they must be hers.

Advise Sue whether she has to take all the bags.

Would it have made any difference if the seller had mistakenly tried to deliver 12 bags of organic fertiliser to Sue instead of mushroom compost?

Answers

1. (a) Amanda's transaction would fall under the Supply of Goods and Services Act 1982. Primarily she is paying for the service of her car and the parts are incidental to the service.

(b) Clive's transaction comes under the Sale of Goods Act 1979. As it is a part exchange deal he is swapping one computer for another and providing a money consideration to make up the price of the new computer.

(c) Farinda's transaction does not fall within the 1979 Act or the 1982 Act provisions. She is buying the furniture on hire purchase and this is not dealt with by either Act. Her transaction would be regulated by the Consumer Credit Act 1974.

(d) George's rental of the video comes under the 1982 Act.

(e) Edwin's purchase of the painting from the gallery is a straightforward sale of goods and comes under 1979 Act. If Edwin wanted 'Fleet' to paint a special painting for him, which could not be bought in the gallery, then the transaction would become a 1982 Act matter. Edwin would be paying for Fleet's services as an artist and the painting he finally acquired would be the goods that go with the service.

2. Anne would appear to be a consumer buying goods from a business seller therefore she has the full protection of the implied terms under the Sale of Goods Act 1979. This means that a breach of an implied term allows the buyer to repudiate the contract as the term is treated as a condition.

   (a) Although the machine works it is not of satisfactory quality under s. 14(2) of the 1979 Act. The appearance and finish of the goods can be taken into account when considering satisfactory quality and the reasonable person would not expect a new washing machine to be scratched.

   The case of *Rogers* v *Parish (Scarborough) Ltd* (1987) can be cited as an example.

   (b) As the machine does not work it is neither of satisfactory quality (s. 14(2)) nor fit for its purpose (s. 14(3)). Even trivial defects can render goods unfit so the fact that this fault can be easily mended does not affect the outcome. It would be unnecessary for Anne to state why she wanted the machine as the purpose is obvious.

   (c) As the defect was pointed out to Anne before she bought the machine she cannot claim that it is not of satisfactory quality now she has acquired the goods. However, if there are any other defects which she was not told of and didn't see herself, she could complain about the quality of the goods on these grounds.

   (d) If the machine is making grinding noises it is probably not of satisfactory quality and if it is affecting the way the machine performs it may even render the item unfit for its purpose. The safety and durability of the product may be questioned. The seller's allegations that she has had the machine for two weeks and therefore has kept it too long to reject it are unlikely to be accepted. As Anne has not used the machine in the first two weeks of ownership she has an opportunity to examine the goods and that would mean being able to try it out. How long you retain the goods before you lose the right to reject them must be judged in relation to the product and what is deemed reasonable.

3. This question deals with whether the lawnmower is in a deliverable state and whether the ownership of the goods has passed from seller to buyer. Even though the lawnmower can be described as specific goods it is not in a deliverable state until the new tyres are fitted and Donald is told it is ready to collect. As the seller had not done a pre-delivery check, it could not be described as being in a deliverable state. Therefore, when it is damaged, it is still in the ownership of the seller and the seller must bear the risk.

4. This question is about buyer's and seller's rights and duties as to delivery of contract goods. The seller must deliver the correct goods in the correct quantity. As the seller has delivered a larger quantity it is up to Sue to decide whether she accepts all the bags and pays for them at the contract rate, or only takes the number of bags she ordered and pays for those at the agreed rate. Alternatively, she can reject the entire consignment and tell the seller she does not want any of them.

   If the seller delivers the right quantity of bags but delivers the wrong product, Sue could reject the goods because under s. 13 of the Sale of Goods Act 1979 they do not fit their description.

Crucial reading and research

Atiyah, *Sale of Goods*, 9th edn., Pitman.

Keenan and Riches, *Business Law*, 6th edn., Longman, Chapter 10.

Kelly and Holmes, *Business Law*, 3rd edn., Cavendish, Chapter 9.

CHAPTER 4

TORT

Chapter summary

This chapter describes how liability principally based upon fault can give rise to a civil claim known as a *tort*. There are a number of torts but the most important is the tort of negligence which is dealt with in some detail.

Studying this chapter will help you to:

- understand and use the various legal terms and cases appropriate to the tort of negligence;

- recognise and use the appropriate tests to establish whether an act of negligence has been committed;

- identify the limitations the courts place upon the duty of care and know why it is important to recognise these;

- apply the legal rules to case based problems.

Assessment targets

Target 1: identifying a valid legal claim in negligence
In a problem question based in negligence you are likely to be asked to discuss whether a claimant has a valid legal claim in negligence. Exercise 1 at the end of this chapter will assess your ability to apply the appropriate legal rules to a problem in order to establish whether a claimant would have a case.

Target 2: recognising different types of negligence claims
You will be asked to consider the different types of negligence claims that may arise and identify their particular features. Exercise 2 at the end of this chapter will check if you can do this.

Target 3: understanding key cases and terms
You have to understand the key cases and terms relating to negligence. Exercise 3 at the end of this chapter will see whether you have grasped these concepts.

Crucial terms, cases and Acts

Tort of negligence
Donoghue v *Stevenson* (1932)
Proximate
Reasonable foreseeability
Fair and reasonable
Limits to the duty of care
Spartan Steel & Alloys Ltd v *Martin & Co. Ltd* (1972)
Hedley Byrne & Co. Ltd v *Heller & Partners Ltd* (1963)
McLoughlin v *O'Brian* (1982)
The reasonable person test
The degree of care against the likelihood of risk

Take your victim as you find him
The costs and practicability of taking precautions
When it is acceptable to take risk
Res ipsa loquitur
When damages are recoverable
Chain of causation (the but for test)
Actions which may break the chain of causation
Remoteness of damage
The Wagon Mound (1961)
Contributory negligence
Volenti non fit injuria
The Consumer Protection Act 1987

Relevant links

Consumer protection is featured in **Chapter 3**. Unfair contract terms are referred to in **Chapter 2**.

Section 1	Introduction to tort

What are you studying?
This section defines what a tort is and outlines the three things that a claimant has to show in order to be successful in a claim in the tort of negligence.

How will you be assessed on this?
An examination question will rarely be limited to these topics alone. You will need to know how to define negligence and how to identify the three things that a claimant has to show in order to be successful in a negligence claim.

What is a tort?

A *tort* is a wrongful act against an individual or a body corporate and his or her property that gives rise to a civil claim, usually resulting in damages being paid to the injured party.

To understand the nature of tort liability it is necessary to appreciate that the defendant (the person committing the wrongful act) does not necessarily intend to cause harm or damage to the claimant (the person who is injured), nor is the motive of the defendant necessarily a factor in deciding if a tort has been committed. The basis of the wrongdoing is based upon the obligations people owe to one another in society.

It is quite possible when a tort is committed that other legal proceedings may also arise. For example, if a person driving a vehicle along a highway whilst under the influence of alcohol knocks down a cyclist (the claimant) then the cyclist may make a civil claim under the tort of negligence against the motorist if the cyclist is hurt and/or his bicycle is damaged. Meanwhile, the police may arrive at the scene of the accident and breathalise the motorist and if the motorist has drunk more alcohol than that allowed under the legal limit a prosecution for a drink driving offence may follow. Thus there can be two actions arising out of the one incident: a civil claim and a criminal action.

Generally tort claims are based upon fault and the most important of these is the tort of negligence but there are a variety of other torts. For example, tort liability for premises, nuisance, defamation, goodwill and business reputations and employer's liability for employees.

Crucial concept   **Tort of negligence.** This is a breach of a legal duty to take care resulting in the unintended harm to the claimant. To establish a case and be successful in a claim in negligence the injured party must prove on the balance of probabilities three things in the following order:
- that the defendant owed the claimant a legal duty of care;
- that the defendant was in breach of that duty;
- that damage has resulted.

Quick test

What must the claimant prove in order to bring a successful claim in negligence against the defendant?

Section 2   The duty of care

What are you studying?

Before the claimant can consider any claim against a defendant, he must show that the defendant owes him a duty of care. This section shows how a duty of care can be established. The duty of care has been limited in certain circumstances and these are also discussed in this section.

How will you be assessed on this?

As a part of an examination question you must be able to identify when a duty of care exists. In doing so you would need to consider proximity, reasonable foreseeability and whether it is fair and reasonable to impose a duty of care. You must also be able to identify situations where the duty of care is limited or excluded.

When a duty of care exists

> **Crucial case** | ***Donoghue v Stevenson* (1932).** A lady went into a café with her friend who bought her a bottle of ginger beer. After she had drunk about half of the bottle she poured the remainder of the drink into her glass and found it contained a decomposed snail. She suffered nervous shock and became ill with gastro-enteritis. She sued Stevenson, the manufacturer of the drink, for negligence. By a majority the House of Lords held that the manufacturer did owe Mrs Donoghue a duty of care because as the consumer of the drink she was someone who might reasonably be expected to be affected by the way the manufacturer made the product.
>
> The most important point to come out of this case is a statement by Lord Atkin that lays down a basic test to establish whether a legal duty of care has arisen:
>
> You must take reasonable care to avoid acts or omissions which you could reasonably foresee would be likely to injure your neighbour. Who then in law is my neighbour? . . . any person so closely and directly affected by my act that I ought to reasonably have then in contemplation as being so affected when I am directing my mind to the acts and omissions which are called in to question.

Obviously not everyone can be classed as your neighbour for the purposes of a negligence claim. In the above case, Mrs Donoghue could be classed as a 'neighbour' in the terms indicated by Lord Atkin because she was a person who might be reasonably affected by the manufacturer's actions as she was the consumer of the product.

> **Crucial tip** | The claimant does not need to have any contractual relationship with the defendant to bring a claim under the tort of negligence. Mrs Donoghue did not buy the ginger beer so she has no contract with the seller and so could not sue the café owner for breach of contract (see Chapter 2). Her friend who bought the ginger beer and did have a contract with the seller could not sue because she did not suffer any damage.

Someone who is likely to be seen as a 'neighbour' in legal terms would have to be said to be sufficiently proximate.

> **Crucial concept** | **Proximate.** There must be a close enough relationship between the defendant and the claimant at the time of the incident.

In Lord Atkin's terms that would mean somebody who would be closely and directly affected by the defendant's actions. So, for example, going back to the cyclist referred to earlier, it could be said that if the drunken driver had been thinking clearly she would have realised that carelessness on her part may have caused damage to the cyclist who was another legitimate road user using that same stretch of road at the same time as her.

Not only must the claimant be owed a duty of care and be proximate it must be reasonably foreseeable that harm could be caused to him.

> **Crucial concept** **Reasonable foreseeability.** It must be demonstrated that the claimant was vulnerable to the risk created by the defendant.

Once again it was reasonably foreseeable that the cyclist might be injured if the drunken motorist was not in proper control of her vehicle as the cyclist was clearly in the vicinity of the motorist and travelling along the same stretch of road at the same time.

However, there is one final question that must be asked before a claimant can establish that there is a legal duty of care owed. Would it be fair and reasonable in all the circumstances to impose a duty of care upon the defendant?

> **Crucial concept** **What is fair and reasonable?** There may be reasons of policy, which would restrict or limit the duty of care owed to another.

For example, in *Hill v Chief Constable of West Yorkshire* (1990), the mother of the last victim of the Yorkshire Ripper alleged that the police had failed to take reasonable care in apprehending the murderer because they had interviewed him before her daughter was murdered and let him go. The Court considered that for policy reasons it would be inappropriate to allow the existence of a duty of care because if such a duty did exist it may lead to public bodies such as the police and fire service being limited in their discretion as to how best to deploy their resources and therefore distract them from their overall statutory duties which are owed to the public in general.

> **Crucial tip** To establish if a duty of care is owed to a person you should go through the three factors which are mentioned above: proximity; reasonable foreseeability; and fair and reasonable.

Limits to the duty of care

> **Crucial concept** **Limits to the duty of care.** To avoid a large number of claims by potential claimants the duty of care has been limited or excluded in certain situations. These include cases of:
> - pure economic loss;
> - negligent misstatements;
> - nervous shock.

PURE ECONOMIC LOSS

While it is possible to make a claim for economic loss resulting from physical injury to a person or damage to property, it is not usually possible to make a claim for pure economic or financial loss. This point is illustrated by reference to the following case.

> **Crucial case** ***Spartan Steel & Alloys Ltd v Martin & Co. Ltd* (1972).** The defendants negligently damaged a cable which supplied power to the claimant's factory. Metal in the furnace was spoilt and the factory was unable to function for some hours. The claimants were able to recover for the spoilt metal and the profit that would have been made from the sale of it. They were unable to recover for loss from further melts which would have been processed as this amounted to pure economic loss.

Crucial tip	Loss for metal spoilt in the furnace was *economic loss* and *was* recoverable.
	Loss of profit on that metal was *consequential economic loss* and *was* recoverable.
	Loss of profit for metal which would have been made was *pure economic loss* and *was not* recoverable.

In limited circumstances a claim for pure economic loss may be successful if it arises as a result of a negligent misstatement.

NEGLIGENT MISSTATEMENTS

It is possible to suffer damage if a party acts upon negligent advice. For example, a client may have a claim against a solicitor who gives him negligent legal advice. In theory a large number of people could be affected by one person's words and so the courts have attempted to limit situations where a duty of care is owed.

Crucial case	***Hedley Byrne & Co. Ltd v Heller & Partners Ltd (1963).*** Hedley Byrne were advertising agents. They were given a reference by Heller & Partners, who were merchant bankers, about the credit worthiness of a third party with whom they wished to do business. They relied upon this reference and placed contracts with the third party but suffered financial loss when it went into liquidation. Hedley Byrne sued Heller for the amount of the loss. They were unsuccessful in their action because of an exclusion clause in the reference. However, the majority of the judges felt that without the clause the claim could have been successful.
	To avoid a mass of legal claims the House of Lords in this case said that for a duty of care to exist in cases of negligent misstatements:
	• there must be a special relationship between the parties (e.g. a professional and his client);
	• the maker of the statement must know that the other party will rely upon his advice and know the use to which it will be put;
	• it must be reasonable in the circumstances for the claimant to rely upon that advice.

Crucial tip	There doesn't need to be a contract between the parties for the claimant to have a case.

The duty of care was limited even further in the case of *Caparo Industries plc v Dickman* (1990). The defendants were a firm of accountants who audited the accounts of Fidelity Plc. They inaccurately represented the financial position of Fidelity and, as a result, the claimants who were existing shareholders bought more shares in the company. They subsequently made a loss and tried to claim against the auditors. It was held that although the auditors owed a duty of care to shareholders to enable them to perform their duty as members of the company, they did not owe a duty of care to them as individuals who might use their advice in buying shares. Thus a huge number of potential claimants were excluded from future claims for inaccurate investment advice. According to Lord Bridge:

. . . auditors of a public company's accounts owe no duty of care to members of the public who rely on the accounts in deciding to buy shares in the company. If the duty of care were owed so widely, it is difficult to see any reason why it should not equally extend to all who rely on the accounts in relation to other dealings with a company as lenders or merchants extending credit to the company.

NERVOUS SHOCK

It is possible for a person to make a claim if he has suffered no personal injury but has suffered nervous shock as a result of another person's negligence. The courts have been cautious in awarding damages and it has been established that the shock suffered must be in the form of a medically recognisable illness. In addition, the injury must have been reasonably foreseeable and there must have been sufficient proximity between the claimant and the defendant.

Crucial case	*McLoughlin* v *O'Brian* (1982). The husband and two children of the claimant were badly injured and a third child was killed in an accident caused by the defendant's negligence. The claimant was not a witness to the accident. She arrived at the hospital one hour later where she witnessed horrific injuries to her family. As a result of the shock she suffered psychiatric illness. Even though she only witnessed the aftermath of the accident, it was held that there was sufficient proximity and it was reasonably foreseeable that she would suffer such an illness.

Crucial tip	Proximity does not mean that the claimant has to be a witness to the incident. In some circumstances witnessing the aftermath may be sufficient.

Quick test

1. What is a 'neighbour' for the purposes of establishing a duty of care?
2. What are the three factors that help establish whether a duty of care exists?
3. In what situations have the courts limited or excluded the extent of the duty of care?

Section 3	Breach of the duty of care

What are you studying?

This section shows how the claimant can establish that the defendant has broken his duty of care.

How will you be assessed on this?

In an examination question, in addition to establishing whether a duty of care exists, you must be able to show how the defendant has broken any duty owed. You must also be able to describe the tests used to show such a breach.

Once you can prove satisfactorily that a duty of care exists, it is important to go on to the next step and prove that a breach of that duty has occurred. Proving that the duty has been broken requires application of another set of tests. It is important to examine each of these in turn so that you do not miss any vital points.

As with Section 1 where you would establish that a duty of care exists, you would need to know if a defendant has broken that duty. You cannot make the assumption that once a duty of care is proved there must be a breach of that duty just because the claimant has suffered injury. So once again you would need to go through the tests to prove there has been a breach of duty.

The basic test that was laid down in a case in 1856 in *Blyth* v *Birmingham Waterworks Co.* is still applicable:

> The defendant . . . fails to do something which a reasonable man guided upon those considerations which ordinarily regulate the conduct of human affairs would do, or does something which a prudent and reasonable man would not do.

Crucial concept   **The reasonable person test.** This is an objective test which would be judged through the eyes of a reasonable person.

For example, would a reasonable contractor dig a hole in the middle of a public pathway and then go off in the evening leaving the hole unfenced and unlit? It could be said that those are not the actions of a reasonable contractor who we would expect to provide a reasonable level of protection against reasonably foreseeable accidents.

Once again the courts will take into account a range of factors which will help them decide if there has been a breach of duty in a given case.

Crucial concept   **Balancing the degree of care against the likelihood of risk.** The greater the risk of injury occurring the more care would be needed. A lesser degree of risk would reduce the degree of care needed.

For example, if you play cricket at a ground that is unfenced and near a road which carries heavy traffic then there is a reasonably high degree of risk that you will hit the ball out of the ground and perhaps injure road users. However, if the ground is fenced in and has high fencing, the risk is considerably reduced. In the first instance any absence of preventative measures would probably mean there is a breach of duty, but in the second instance the precautions taken weighed against the likelihood of someone being hit may mean that a claimant would fail.

Crucial concept   **'Take your victim as you find him'.** If the claimant is quite young, elderly or less able-bodied than the average person the degree of care may need to be increased to a standard that would protect him.

It is no good the defendant saying the precautions he took were adequate for the average able-bodied adult if the type of person who may be put at risk is not in that category of person.

It would be no good a defendant saying he put up warning notices outside his premises saying that the floor was slippery because it had just been polished if the premises were attended by a blind person who clearly could not read the notice. That would not stop the defendant being in breach of his duty.

> **Crucial concept** **Assess the cost and practicality of taking precautions to reduce risk factors.** It is acceptable for a defendant to consider the cost of taking preventative measures and the practicality of being able to reduce the risk. A balance has to be struck between the measures that would have to be taken to avoid foreseeable harm and the likelihood of that risk occurring.

Of course if the costs and the practical steps necessary are not unreasonable and the risk factors could be reduced, the defendant who fails to take appropriate action is likely to be in breach of his duty. Perhaps it would be worth the defendant asking what the reasonable person in his position would have done.

> **Crucial concept** **When it is acceptable to take risk.** Assess the social utility and importance of the defendant's actions.

Sometimes the defendant's actions at a given time may be of crucial importance to the community and therefore justify the taking of risks that would not be thought acceptable in normal circumstances. In a life and death situation a fire crew, an ambulance or a police car may take risks that would not under normal circumstances be considered acceptable.

> **Crucial tip** If a defendant wants to show that he exercised a proper degree of care in a particular instance, it may assist his case to show that he was following commonly accepted practices or industry standards, or if he was a professional person that he was exercising his skills to the standard of the reasonable professional in that job. For example, the reasonable doctor, lawyer, vet, engineer, etc.

> **Crucial concept** *Res ipsa loquitur.* This means 'the thing speaks for itself'.

> **Crucial tip** Do not be put off by Latin phrases – it is more important to understand the principle behind a phrase than to be able to remember the Latin.

There may be certain situations where a claimant cannot prove on the balance of probabilities in exactly what way the defendant was negligent. Nevertheless, there may be only one possible explanation for what happened and that is the negligence of the defendant. Where, in this situation, the claimant wants to suggest that 'the thing speaks for itself', the claimant does not have to prove his case; instead the defendant is placed in a position where he has to disprove his negligence. This will only apply if the following three conditions are met:

- the defendant must have been in control of the 'thing' which caused the damage – this does not mean he personally had to be in control, it could be someone working for him for whom he has to take responsibility;

- the accident could not have normally happened without there having been negligence – if there are other possible explanations as to how the accident may have happened then *res ipsa loquitur* will fail;

- the cause of the accident must be unknown – if the defendant can put forward some other reasonable explanation as to why the accident happened the claim will fail.

For example, if a supermarket customer slips due to a yoghurt spillage in one of the aisles in the store and is hurt, it is up to the store to show that the accident did not occur due to lack of care on its part. It would be up to the defendant to show that in the ordinary course of events this kind of accident does not happen if the floors are kept clean and spillages are dealt with as soon as they occur. It is up to the defendant to provide the evidence as to what happened and if he cannot do so the claimant can say 'the thing speaks for itself'.

Crucial tip	When faced with a negligence question do not assume you can use *res ipsa loquitur* just because it looks obvious to you that the defendant is at fault. Go through the tests to see if you can prove negligence in the normal way first. If that fails, look to *res ipsa loquitur*.

Quick test

1. What is the test for establishing whether a breach of duty exists?
2. What factors would increase or decrease the degree of care owed by a defendant?
3. When is it possible to use *res ipsa loquitur*?

Section 4   Resultant damage

What are you studying?

The claimant must show that the breach of the duty of care by the defendant has resulted in damage. This section covers tests used to determine whether the damage suffered is a direct consequence of the defendant's breach.

How will you be assessed on this?

In an examination question, in addition to establishing whether a duty of care exists and whether the duty has been broken you will need to show the resultant damage. You will also need to consider the chain of causation, whether that chain has been broken and whether the damage which occurred is too remote a consequence of that breach.

Crucial concept	**When damages are recoverable.** The claimant can only recover damages if he can prove the defendant owed him a duty of care which was broken and that breach of duty caused the damage.

In order to test whether the defendant's negligence was the cause of the claimant's injury it is useful to apply the 'but for' test.

Crucial concept	**Chain of causation (the 'but for' test).** This test states 'but for' the defendant's actions the damage would not have occurred. This is also known as a chain of causation. Thus if the claimant would have suffered the damage irrespective of what the defendant did or failed to do, the damage is not caused by the defendant's breach.

For example, a person attends an accident and emergency department at a hospital complaining of feeling ill and he has been poisoned but the hospital fail to detect this. If the person dies, is the hospital negligent? If the person would have died anyhow no matter whether the hospital had detected the problem and treated it, the hospital is not liable for the person's death. Whatever the hospital did or did not do would not have changed the outcome.

Crucial tip	Do not forget that it is up to the claimant to show that the defendant's negligence materially contributed to the injury/damage. Where there are a number of possible causes for the injury/damage, it will be very difficult for the claimant to show that it was entirely the defendant's fault.

Crucial concept	**Actions which may break the chain of causation.** Where there is evidence that the defendant is liable for damage to the claimant it does not necessarily follow that he should be liable for all the damage that the claimant suffers. There may be a break in the 'chain of causation' which is caused by some intervening act.

For example, some totally unforeseen natural event such as a flash flood or some third party's actions may cause further damage or even the claimant himself may do something unreasonable (for example, jump down a flight of stairs with a broken leg caused by an earlier incident).

However, if the intervening act did not materially affect or contribute to the damage, or could have been expected in the circumstances, the defendant's acts or omissions will still be the direct cause of the damage. So, for example, assume a claimant is injured at work, due to negligence on the part of his employer and his employer admits liability. The claimant has to go to hospital following the injury and is given an anti-tetanus injection which is usual in the circumstances. The injection produces a rare and unforeseen complication that leads to a permanent disability. Could the original defendant say that the hospital's administration of the anti-tetanus injection was an intervening act and broke the chain of causation? It is unlikely that the defendant would succeed as it is standard practice to administer an anti-tetanus injection following the type of injury the claimant suffered and even if the doctor had tested for allergic reactions this would have not shown up. Therefore the original defendant remains liable for the claimant's injuries.

Crucial concept	**Remoteness of damage.** Was the damage that occurred too remote? The defendant cannot necessarily be held responsible for all the damage that may occur following a breach of duty. The damage must be of a type which was reasonably foreseeable following the breach of duty.

Crucial tip	When considering what is reasonably foreseeable ask what the reasonable person might have imagined would be the result of the breach of duty by the claimant.

Crucial case	**The _Wagon Mound_ (1961).** The defendants negligently allowed oil to spill from their vessel into Sydney harbour. Some of the oil ended up beneath the claimant's wharf where some welding work was taking place. On spotting the oil the welders stopped work to check whether it was safe to continue welding. They were assured that the oil would not catch fire so they resumed welding. What they did not know was that some old cotton rags that had fallen into the oily water had caught fire. This ignited oil and the resultant fire destroyed the wharf.
	Clearly the defendants were in breach of their duty for having discharged the oil from the ship but were not liable for the fire that ultimately damaged the wharf. The reason for this was because whilst it was foreseeable that the wharf would be damaged by the fouling from the oil, it was not foreseeable that it would be damaged by fire. (The oil had a high ignition point and it was not likely that it would ignite in water.)

Once the type of damage is reasonably foreseeable it does not matter how it actually occurred or how severe the damage turns out to be, the defendant will still be liable. Therefore if the foreseeable type of damage may be burns, it is irrelevant that the injuries are caused by an explosion instead of by fire. It is equally irrelevant that the damage turns out to be far more severe than was expected.

Quick test
1. What is the link between the defendant's actions and the damage caused?
2. What tests should always be checked for?

Section 5	**Defences to a claim for negligence**

What are you studying?

This section covers the defences that may be available to the defendant in a claim for negligence. The defendant's liability for a negligent act may be reduced or limited if one of these defences is raised. Note, however, that a defendant cannot exempt himself from liability resulting in a claimant's personal injury or death if these consequences are caused by negligence in a business context (see Chapter 2: s. 2(2), Unfair Contract Terms Act 1977).

How will you be assessed on this?

You may be asked to describe the defences available to a defendant in an action for negligence or you may be expected to pick out possible defences as part of a problem question.

Crucial concept	**Contributory negligence.** Where the claimant is found to have contributed in some way through his own fault to his injury, the amount of damages that would have been awarded to him may be reduced to an extent that the court thinks appropriate.

This does not relieve the defendant from liability and places the responsibility on the defendant to show that the claimant contributed in some way to his injury. For example, a car passenger who suffers injury in a car accident caused by the driver's negligence may find that the damages recoverable are reduced if it was found that he was not wearing a seat belt. The defendant would probably say that the injuries would have been far less severe if the passenger had worn a seat belt and instead of getting a 100% award the claimant's award may be reduced by 25%.

Crucial concept ***Volenti non fit injuria* (to one who volunteers no harm is done).** A person who consents to run the risk of accidental injury will be prevented from bringing a successful claim in negligence. If a defendant puts forward this defence it can relieve him completely of liability for the claimant's injuries. The defendant would probably have to show that the claimant expressly agreed to run the risk or it was clear by the claimant's conduct.

A leading case which illustrates this is *ICI Ltd* v *Shatwell* (1965), where two brothers employed by ICI as shot firers completely ignored all safety regulation as to testing detonators. One brother was injured by the other's actions. He tried to sue their employer on the grounds of vicarious liability (see Chapter 7 for definition) and breach of statutory duty. He failed in his claim as the employer put forward a complete defence of '*volenti*'. The employer was able to show that the brother had not only agreed to ignore the safety rules but had willingly taken part in the scheme.

Crucial tip If contributory negligence is made out, damages will be reduced by the amount that the court thinks the claimant is to blame. If '*volenti*' is made out, the claimant will receive no damages.

The courts do not like defendants using the complete defence of '*volenti*' unless there is very clear evidence that the injured person knew of and consented to run the risk of injury. It is far more likely that the courts would accept a partial defence of contributory negligence.

Quick test

1. What defences are available to the defendant in a claim for negligence?

Section 6 | Fault-based liability and strict liability

What are you studying?
This section outlines the differences between fault-based liability and strict liability. It considers liability for defective products under the Consumer Protection Act 1987.

How will you be assessed on this?
You may be asked a problem question where you have to consider who is liable when a person suffers death, injury or loss as a result of a defective product.

In order to claim damages in negligence it has already been stated that the claimant must show that the defendant was at fault – that he owed a duty of care to the claimant, that he broke that duty and that damage has resulted.

In some cases liability is said to be 'strict'. This means that the claimant does not have to show any fault by the defendant for the damage that the claimant has suffered. An example of strict liability is when an employer is vicariously liable for the torts of his employee. Another example is liability for defective products under Part I of the Consumer Protection Act 1987, although some lawyers may argue that because there are defences available to the defendant, it is not really strict liability.

Crucial concept	**The Consumer Protection Act 1987.** Part I of the Act imposes liability on a party for damage suffered by a consumer as a result of a product being defective. Damage includes personal injury, death and loss or damage to private property that exceeds £275. The product must have been supplied in the course of a business and so a private sale would not be included.

All the claimant has to show is:

- that he has suffered damage as a result of a defect in a product;

- that the defendant was the producer, own brander or importer of that product.

What is a defective product?
The definition in s. 1 of the Act includes a wide range of products. It can include components of other products, raw materials and abstracted items such as electricity. It does not include agricultural produce.

Section 3 says that the product is defective if it is unsafe. Obviously to make a claim under the Act, the product must also have caused some damage. All circumstances are taken into account including the manner and purpose for which the product has been marketed, the normal use of the product and the safety standard applicable at the time it was supplied.

Crucial tip	Although, for example, a table knife may be considered unsafe and may cause injury, a claim against the manufacturer would fail as the court would take into account the purpose for which the product had been marketed.

Who is the defendant?
Those who may be liable are:

- The producer – this is the person who manufactures, abstracts or processes the product.

- The own brander – this is the person who puts his own name or brand on the product.

- The importer – this is the person who first imports the product into the European Union.

- The supplier – the supplier will only be liable if upon request from the claimant, he fails within a reasonable time to identify the importer or producer of the product.

What defences are available to the defendant?
The following are available:

- That the defect occurred because the defendant had complied with EU or UK laws or obligations. For example, safety regulations may require that the product contains a particular substance which is later found to be harmful.

- That the defendant did not supply the product to another. For example, it may have been stolen from him.

- That the product was not supplied in the course of a business, nor was it supplied for profit. For example, a home-made gift.

- That the defect did not exist in the product at the time it was supplied. For example, it may have become defective because it was stored incorrectly by the retailer.

- The development risks defence. This is that the state of scientific knowledge at the time the product was produced was not such that the producer might have been expected to discover the defect.

- If the product was a raw material or a component of another product, the defect was a result of the design of the other product or was attributable to compliance with instructions provided by the producer of the other product.

What is not included?
The following is not included as part of a claim:

- business loss;

- damage to property worth less than £275;

- loss or damage to the product itself;

- pure economic loss.

> Crucial tip
>
> If the claimant does not fall within the category of those who can make a claim under the Consumer Protection Act 1987 he must make a claim in common law negligence.

Quick test

1. What is strict liability?
2. What does a claimant have to show if he wishes to bring a claim for damage suffered as the result of a defective product?
3. Who may be liable under the Consumer Protection Act 1987?
4. What defences are available to the defendant?

Crucial examples

1. June is the passenger in the front seat of Jack's car. She is not wearing a seatbelt. As they travel through the centre of town at 45 mph, a motorcyclist pulls out of a side turning. June is injured in the resulting collision. Discuss who may be liable to June in a claim in negligence and what she must prove in any such claim.

2. (a) Explain in what situations the duty of care has been limited.
   (b) When may a person bring a claim under Part I of the Consumer Protection Act 1987?

3. (a) Explain the importance of the following cases:

   - *Donoghue* v *Stevenson;*

   - *Spartan Steel & Alloys Ltd* v *Martin & Co. Ltd;*

   - *Hedley Byrne & Co. Ltd* v *Heller & Partners Ltd;*

   - *McLoughlin* v *O'Brian.*

   (b) Explain the following terms:

   - *res ipsa loquitur;*

   - the 'but for' test;

- remoteness of damage;
- contributory negligence;
- *volenti non fit injuria.*

Answers

1. In this question you would need to define negligence and to discuss who owes a duty of care to whom, whether it has been broken and whether damage has occurred. You would need to consider causation and remoteness of damage. It is possible that both Jack and the motorcyclist may be liable. Jack has broken the speed limit and the motorcyclist has pulled out of a side turning. June may decide to sue either or both of them. You must also consider whether any defences are available to the defendants. As June is not wearing her seatbelt, there may be contributory negligence and her damages will be reduced accordingly.

2. (a) The duty of care has been limited in a number of situations. These include cases of economic loss, negligent misstatements and nervous shock. These are explained in more detail in Section 2 of this chapter.

   (b) A person may bring a claim under Part I of the Consumer Protection Act 1987 for damage suffered as a result of a product being defective. Liability is strict and there is no need for the consumer to prove fault. Business loss is not included and neither is loss or damage to the product itself. Damage to property worth less than £275 is also not included and pure economic loss cannot be recovered. See Section 6 of this chapter for more details.

3. (a) *Donoghue v Stevenson* established that you owe a duty of care to anyone who may be affected by your acts or omission to act.

   Spartan Steel & Alloys v Martin & Co. Ltd established that in a claim for personal injury or damage to property in tort, pure economic loss is not recoverable.

   Hedley Byrne & Co. Ltd v Heller & Partners Ltd established limits to the duty of care in cases of negligent misstatement.

   McLoughlin v O'Brian established that it is possible to make a claim for nervous shock provided that the damage is reasonably foreseeable and there is sufficient proximity between the defendant and the claimant. Witnessing the aftermath of an accident may amount to sufficient proximity.

   (b) *Res ipsa loquitur* means the thing speaks for itself. If you cannot prove how the defendant was negligent but there is only one explanation for what has happened the claimant may be able to establish *res ipsa loquitur*.

   The 'but for' test is used to establish whether the defendant's negligence was the cause of the claimant's injury.

   If the damage that occurred was too remote a consequence of the breach, the defendant cannot be held liable.

   Contibutory negligence is where a claimant has through his own fault contributed to his injury. His damages will be reduced accordingly.

   If a person consents to the risk of injury he will not have a successful claim in negligence.

Crucial reading and research

Harpwood, *Principles of Tort Law,* 4th edn., Cavendish.

Hepple, Howard and Matthews, *Tort, Cases and Materials,* 5th edn., Butterworths.

Stephenson, *Sourcebook on Torts,* 2nd edn., Cavendish.

CHAPTER 5

ORGANISATIONS

Chapter summary

This chapter explores the various types of business mediums that allow people to carry on trades and businesses. It considers the characteristics of various business organisations and the advantages and disadvantages of trading in each. It describes how each of these business organisations is set up and what legal regulations would govern their operation. Finally it considers what the legal implications would be if they ceased to trade and became insolvent.

Studying this Chapter will help you to:

- identify the most common types of business organisations;

- recognise the advantages and disadvantages of trading under different types of business organisations;

- become familiar with the legal requirements necessary to set up and operate different business organisations;

- be aware of the consequences when a business ceases to trade.

Assessment targets

Target 1: defining concepts

You must be able to explain the differences between corporate and unincorporated bodies and limited and unlimited liability. Exercise 1 at the end of this chapter will check whether you can do this.

Target 2: defining business organisations

You must be able to outline the main characteristics of the three most common types of business organisations. To do this you will have to look at the features which distinguish one business organisation from another. Exercise 2 at the end of this chapter will test whether you can recognise the features appropriate to each type of business.

Target 3: naming a business

You must be able to identify the rules relating to choosing a name for a business and be able to apply them. Exercise 3 at the end of this chapter will check whether you can identify and apply the appropriate rules.

Target 4: choosing an appropriate business organisation

You must be able to choose an appropriate business organisation to fit the requirements of the parties referred to in a problem question and then explain why it is appropriate to their needs. Exercise 4 at the end of this chapter will test whether you can pick the right type of business organisation and justify your choice.

Crucial terms, cases and Acts

Sole traders
Partnerships
Registered companies
Salomon v Salomon and Co. Ltd (1897)
Choosing a business name
Passing off
Sole trader's property
Partnership name
Partnership property
Partnership finance
Partners as agents
Joint and several liability
Company name
Company property

Company finance
Company ownership and management
Goodwill
Bankruptcy
Individual voluntary arrangement
Partnership dissolution
Partnership insolvency
Voluntary arrangements and administration
 orders
Members' voluntary winding up
Creditors' voluntary winding up
Compulsory winding up
Company voluntary arrangements and
 administration orders

Relevant links

Company law is dealt with in greater depth in **Chapter 6**.

Section 1	Classification of business organisations

What are you studying?

In this section the different types of business organisations under which businesses may operate are identified.

How will you be assessed on this?

You should be able to identify key concepts such as corporate and unincorporated bodies and distinguish between public and private sector organisations. Questions may require you to demonstrate an awareness of the three main types of business organisations and identify who would choose to operate under each of these systems.

Business is a very general term but most people understand it to mean some sort of commercial enterprise which will generate a profit for its owners by marketing its goods and services. Not all types of organisations which are run as businesses are conducted along these lines. Charities, local authorities and government departments can trade and carry on a business but do not seek to make profits for their owners or members. Perhaps the only common characteristic that all these organisations share is that they trade and have to abide by trading rules.

Common characteristics of most business organisations

Most business organisations have the following characteristics:

- **Defined business aims and objectives.** Most business organisations are set up for a specific purpose. Some may evolve in a commercial environment while others may be limited as to what they can do by regulatory provisions, for example, charities and public sector organisations.

- **A clear organisational structure.** There will be evidence of a system of organisation and management.

- **Accountability.** The organisation will be accountable to those who own it. Those who manage the organisation will be accountable for running it. The organisation itself will be accountable to those it employs and those with whom it trades.

Categories

Business organisations can be roughly categorised under the following headings:

- corporate and unincorporated bodies;
- public and private sector organisations.

Corporate and unincorporated bodies

A *corporate* body is usually a group of individuals who have joined together for a common purpose and have by legal incorporation created an artificial legal person with a separate legal identity from themselves.

An *unincorporated* body can be an individual such as a sole trader or a group of individuals such as a partnership who form together for a common business purpose.
In the eyes of the law the body they operate under does not have a distinct legal personality separate from them.

Public and private sector organisations

Public sector organisations are usually created under Acts of Parliament. For example, local authorities are established under the Local Government Act 1972. Public sector organisations are owned and controlled by the State and their primary purpose is to provide public services such as health and housing.

Initially many public sector organisations were set up to provide services to the public on a national basis, often as a monopoly. Most of these organisations have now been returned to the private sector in the form of public limited companies, for example, electricity, water and gas.

Private sector organisations are owned by private individuals or other organisations and are principally concerned with commercial trading. They are not usually created by an Act of Parliament and don't have a monopoly position.

The three most common forms of business organisation are:

- sole traders;
- partnerships;
- registered companies.

> Crucial concept   **Sole traders.** A sole trader is a person operating an unincorporated business and having full responsibility for its management.

Many 'one man' businesses are sole traders. These people may describe themselves as self-employed or working for themselves although they can employ other people. Being a sole trader does not exempt such a business from being subject to the general laws of trading. For example, a sole trader would need to comply with the law regarding the employment of staff, acquiring and operating business premises, tax provisions and sale and supply of goods and services.

> Crucial concept   **Partnerships.** A partnership is the relationship which subsists between persons carrying on a business in common with a view to profit. This is the definition of a partnership as contained within the Partnership Act 1890.

This is still an unincorporated form of business organisation but the persons operating it agree to manage it together and share the profits. A partnership has a number of features in common with sole traders but the business is operated by and for the benefit of all the partners. This form of business organisation is still favoured by professional people working together, for example, doctors, solicitors and accountants.

> Crucial tip   A sole trader who employs others is not in partnership with his employees because he has not agreed to share the profits of the business with them. Those who agree to share the business profits with their fellow partners are in partnership.

> Crucial concept   **Registered companies.** A registered company is a corporate body which has a separate legal identity from its members.

The essential difference between the registered company and the previous two business organisations discussed above is its separate legal identity. Most registered companies are set up as *limited liability companies,* which means that the liability of the member is limited to the extent which he agreed to contribute by way of shares or guarantee. A limited liability company can be a public company or a private company. (For further details regarding public and private companies, see Chapter 6.)

Crucial case	**Salomon v Salomon and Co. Ltd (1897).** Mr Salomon formed a limited company and sold his boot making and repair business to it for £39,000. The new company paid the purchase price by issuing to Mr Salomon £20,000 of shares, (his wife and five children taking only 1 share each) and a £10,000 debenture (a secured loan over the company's assets which would be paid before any unsecured creditors).
	About a year after formation, the company became insolvent owing about £8,000 to its unsecured creditors and only having £6,000 assets. Mr Salomon claimed the £6,000 under his secured loan. The unsecured creditors objected arguing that as he was the owner of the company, in all but name, any money the company had should go towards paying off their debts.
	The House of Lords held that as the company had been properly formed and as there was no evidence of fraud, Mr Salomon could as a secured creditor of the company, claim the £6,000. In the eyes of the law Mr Salomon and the company were two distinct legal persons and he did not owe any personal responsibility for the company's debts over and above his fully paid up shares.

Crucial tip	The liability of company members may be limited but the company as a separate legal personality is fully liable to the extent of its assets.

Quick test

1. What is the difference between a corporate and unincorporated body?
2. Name the three most common forms of business organisations.

Section 2	**The advantages and disadvantages of trading under different types of business organisations**

What are you studying?

Those setting up a business have to decide which is the most appropriate form of business organisation for them. To help them make a choice it is useful to compare and contrast the advantages and disadvantages of operating in each type of organisation.

How will you be assessed on this?

You need to appreciate the differences between the three main types of business organisations so that you could advise someone who wanted to set up in business what would be most appropriate for him. Questions may ask you to do this. Alternatively, you may be asked to identify the advantages and disadvantages of a particular form of business organisation or even compare and contrast the different forms of trading.

The three common forms of trading organisations are sole trader, partnership and limited liability company. Although all of them have some common characteristics and have to observe the same or similar rules, for example pay tax, regulations regarding the sale and supply of goods and services, there are a number of features which set them apart from one another.

These distinguishing factors may help someone setting up in business to decide which is the most appropriate form of business organisation for their type of business.

It is vital that you understand the advantages and disadvantages of each type of business organisation as described below.

Sole traders

ADVANTAGES

- The sole trader has complete control over how he manages his business. He is not accountable to anyone for his commercial decisions.

- The sole trader is entitled to all the profits from his business.

- There are no formalities attached to setting up the business. As soon as the business is created the sole trader can commence trading.

- There is no requirement for a sole trader to open up his financial affairs to public scrutiny.

DISADVANTAGES

- The sole trader has unlimited liability for the debts of the business. This means that if the business fails the sole trader stands to lose virtually all his personal assets and could be made bankrupt.

- Obtaining finance to launch a sole trader's business can be difficult as institutional lenders are reluctant to lend money without being offered security. Therefore raising capital can be restricted and can limit business plans.

> Crucial tip — Lenders require loan guarantees such as a mortgage upon a family home.

Close family members such as spouses or parents who act as guarantors or unsecured lenders for a sole trader's business should be independently advised of the financial risks they are taking. In the event of the sole trader's business failing they would be unlikely to recover their debts.

The sole trader may suffer the stress and worry of having to manage the business and take all the crucial decisions alone. Sole traders who work alone have the added worry that if they are unable to work, due to illness, they cannot earn anything.

A sole trader's business will cease when he retires. Therefore in order to make sure he will be adequately provided for when he retires he must make personal provision for his retirement.

The sole trader form of business is probably best suited to an individual who wants to retain total control over his affairs and who only needs a modest amount of finance to launch his business.

Partnerships

ADVANTAGES

- There are no legal formalities required to set up a partnership. Therefore the partners can carry on any business they choose providing it is legal.

> Crucial tip — Those wishing to run a well-regulated partnership would be well advised to draw up a partnership deed setting out the nature of their business and the rights and responsibilities of the partners.

- The partners can manage their business as they see fit. They can share responsibilities and decision making with fellow partners.

- A partnership will have the benefit of the skills and expertise of its partners. This means that not only are there more people to share the work load but there may be a variety of expertise available amongst the partners.

- The partnership will be financed by the partners putting capital into the business. This means that obtaining finance to start the business will not be entirely dependant upon one person or so heavily reliant upon loans.

- A partnership's financial affairs are not open to public scrutiny.

DISADVANTAGES

- A partnership does not have a separate legal personality distinct from its partners.

- All partners have unlimited liability for the debts of the partnership.

> Crucial concept | A partnership entered into under the *Limited Partnership Act 1907* can offer limited liability to some partners subject to certain restrictions. The *Limited Liability Partnership Act 2000* provides limited liability for partners operating under its rules.

- A partnership will be dissolved upon the death or bankruptcy of a partner or upon a partner giving notice to his fellow partners.

- Every partner is the agent of the partnership and of his fellow partners. This means that one partner will not be able to avoid liability if another partner makes a contract on behalf of the partnership even though the contracting partner had no authority to do so.

> Crucial tip | Because partners can put one another at financial risk it is vitally important that there be trust and good faith between partners.

Partners are obliged to share profits with their fellow partners. In the absence of contrary agreement, all partners get an equal share so even if one partner works harder than another they will all share equally in the rewards.

A partner cannot transfer his interest in the partnership to another person without the consent of his partners who must be willing to enter into a new partnership with the transferee.

Non-professional partnerships are usually limited to 20 members.

Partnerships are favoured by professional people who rely upon one another's good faith and good judgement and do not want their financial affairs subject to public scrutiny. In common with a sole trader, partners share the risk of unlimited liability.

Limited liability companies

ADVANTAGES

- A company is a separate legal entity. This means that the company has a legal identity of its own which is quite separate from its owners. It can own property and make contracts in its own name.

- The liability of company members is limited. Members are only liable to the extent of the amount unpaid on their shares or the amount they have guaranteed in the event of the company winding up.

> **Crucial tip**　In small companies where there are few members who are also the company directors, limited liability may be of little advantage as lenders will only lend money to companies who have sufficient assets to cover their loans. If the company has insufficient assets, the lender will ask the directors to stand as personal guarantors for the loan advanced.

- A company can continue in existence perpetually. This means that if the membership of the company changes or the management alters the company will still continue in existence.

- A company can raise money by creating loans, known as floating charges, over its whole undertaking or a part thereof. For example, it can offer stock and book debts as security. (See Chapter 6 for further details.)

- Members can transfer their shares to whoever they wish. This means that they can leave the company by selling or gifting their shares to someone else.

> **Crucial tip**　In reality this is true for shareholders of public companies but in many small private companies the transfer of shares may be restricted and the directors may have an absolute discretion to refuse to register a transfer.

- A company can have as many members as it wishes. It is possible to have a private single member company!

DISADVANTAGES

- A limited liability company must be registered with the Registrar of Companies, according to the requirements laid down in the *Companies Act 1985*, before it can commence trading.

> **Crucial tip**　It is possible to buy an 'off the shelf' company which is pre-formed to avoid this initial step.

- A company must comply with the formalities laid down under the Companies Act 1985. For example, hold members meetings, conduct certain business by way of resolutions, keep minutes of meetings and publish notices of meetings for members. Some of these formalities have been reduced in recent years especially for smaller private companies.

- A company's affairs are open to public scrutiny. Companies must file annual returns to the Registrar of Companies such as publication of accounts and evidence of an annual audit. These rules have been considerably relaxed in recent years for small private companies.

- A company should only operate in accordance with the objects it has laid out in its memorandum.

> **Crucial tip**　These days it is possible for a company to register its objects as a general trading company which allows it a wide scope of activity.

- A shareholder does not have a right to take part in the management of the company unless he is a member of the Board of Directors.

- A shareholder is not automatically entitled to a share of company profits. A shareholder will only receive a dividend (a share of company profits) if the Board of Directors think the company has made sufficient profits to allow a payment.

Limited liability companies are set up by persons who wish to minimise their financial risks and operate behind the security of a separate legal organisation. However, they have to be prepared to comply with the rules and regulations set out in the Companies Acts.

Quick test

1. What do sole traders and partnerships have in common?
2. What is the differences between unlimited and limited liability?

| Section 3 | **The formation and operation of different types of business organisations** |

What are you studying?

In this section the legal requirements for a sole trader, a partnership and a limited liability company to set up their respective businesses are identified. The similarities and differences that occur in setting up and operating the various business organisations will be considered.

How will you be assessed on this?

It is necessary to be able to identify what legal steps are required to set up as a sole trader, a partnership or a limited liability company. You should be able to identify the issues that the potential trader must consider in each case. Some of these may be common to all three types of business organisations but others may be particularly relevant to only one or two. Questions may ask you to consider features common to all types of business formation or focus on the legal requirement of a particular organisation.

Each type of organisation requires some formalities to be met before it can trade successfully. Some organisations require more detailed planning and need to comply with a greater number of legal requirements than others. As we have seen from the previous section those that seek greater financial security, for example members of limited liability companies, have to fulfil a larger number of pre- and post-formation requirements.

Sole traders

A sole trader requires no formal documentation to set up his business. The self-employed pay income tax under Schedule D and under this method of assessment they can deduct business expenses to obtain tax relief.

| Crucial tip | Taxpayers are required to keep records of their income, expenditure and capital gains so that they can fill in their tax forms. |

The sole trader must comply with the *Business Names Act 1985* if he does not intend to operate under his own name.

| Crucial concept | **Choosing a business name.** When a trader uses any name other than only his surname with or without forenames or initials he is using a business name. |

For example, if Dan Walker a plumber calls his business Dan Walker or D Walker this is not a business name but if he calls his business 'Dan's 24 hour Plumbing Service' this is a business name.

The Business Names Act controls the type of business name a trader can use. He cannot use a name which suggests his business is associated with central or local government, has national or international connections or is associated with specific bodies such as building societies unless the Department of Trade and Industry consent to it. Similarly, he cannot suggest his business is associated with certain registered bodies or organisations unless the relevant organisation consents to it. For example, he would not be able to imply that he had association with a charity or was connected with any professional body such as the Royal College of Nursing unless he had the consent of the relevant body. He cannot use any words in a name that would be obscene or clearly misleading to the public.

The sole trader must display his own name and a contact address on his business documentation and at his business premises if customers and suppliers go there. He must also give this information to anyone he does business with if they ask for it.

Crucial concept	**Passing off.** The sole trader must also make sure that he does not use a name so like that of another similar business that it would confuse the public. This is called passing off. The business already using the name could bring a civil claim in the tort of passing off if this happened.

Crucial tip	As there is no register of business names, a person wishing to use a business name would be wise to check the local yellow pages directory as well as the index of company names and the trade marks index to make sure there is no similar business trading under the same name.

Crucial concept	**Sole trader's property.** Any property transaction the sole trader enters into will be in his own name and he will bear personal liability for it. If he operates from business premises he should check that there are no planning considerations or relevant permissions that he needs to obtain before he can begin trading from them.

Partnerships

A partnership can be set up without the partners entering into a partnership deed but the partnership will be subject to the *Partnership Act 1890*. It is far wiser to have a partnership deed setting out the nature of the business, the capital investment of each partner, the profit share each will receive and the responsibilities and involvement of each partner rather than to leave it to chance. For example, a deed can specify that a sleeping or dormant partner does not take part in the active management of the partnership or a salaried partner does not put capital into the firm and is paid a salary not a profit share.

Partnerships need to keep accounting records otherwise they would not be able to calculate partnership profits, expenses and each partner's profit share. Partnership income is charged to tax under Schedule D. Tax is assessed on the partnership as a whole and then each partner pays a share of the tax bill according to their profit allocation. All partners are jointly liable for the partnership tax bill..

Crucial tip	Salaried partners are regarded as employees and pay tax under Schedule E by the PAYE (pay as you earn) system.

Crucial concept	**Partnership name.** If a partnership does not operate under the surnames (with or without forenames or initials) of all its partners, it is operating under a business name and is subject to the Business Names Act 1985.

For example, if Smith, Brown, White and Jones are partners in a firm and call the firm by their surnames, they are not operating under a business name. However if they decided to call the firm Smiths or Smith, Brown and Co., then this would be classed as a business name.

Crucial tip	If there are less than 20 partners in the firm, all their names must appear on their letterheads; if there are more than 20 partners, then this is unnecessary but their names must be displayed at their business premises.

Crucial concept	**Partnership property.** Property bought with partnership funds or intended to be treated as partnership property is classed as partnership property.

A partnership is not a separate legal entity and therefore it cannot own property. Partnership property must be held by the partners as co-owners or it must be made clear that specific property remains in the personal ownership of a particular partner.

Crucial concept	**Partnership finance.** A partnership is financed by the capital input of the partners.

If the partnership wishes to raise loans the partners will have to secure the loan against the partnership assets or give personal guarantees.

Crucial concept	**Partners as agents.** When conducting partnership business, each partner is the agent of his co-partners and the partnership.

If a partner enters into a contract on behalf of the partnership, he will bind his fellow partners and the partnership to the contract, even if he was not actually authorised to enter into such a deal.

Similarly, if a partner commits a tort in the course of partnership business the other partners would be liable for his actions.

Crucial concept	**Joint and several liability.** Partners are jointly and severally liable for the debts of the firm. This means that the partners can be sued together (jointly) or they can be sued individually (severally). This could result in one partner having to meet partnership debts if the partnership has insufficient funds to pay them.

Limited liability companies

For a more detailed account of the formation and operation of companies, see Chapter 6.

A company must register with the Registrar of Companies before it can begin operating as a limited liability company. It must obtain a certificate of incorporation and it must comply with registration procedures set out in the Companies Act 1985.

The limited liability company's accounts and particulars are open to public inspection and its affairs are monitored annually by the Registrar of Companies. Companies must appoint auditors (although small private companies may not need to comply with this requirement).

Companies pay corporation tax on the profits they make.

Crucial concept	**Company name.** A company must be registered with a company name. This must end with the word 'Limited' (Ltd) if it is a private company and 'Public Limited Company' (plc) if it is public company.

A company cannot adopt a name that is the same as one already registered on the Index of Company Names. A company name will not be registered if it is offensive. Registration will not be permitted unless approval is obtained for names suggesting government association or links with professional bodies or recognised organisations, for example, Home Office or Royal. A company may be required to change its name if it is too like that of another company or it gives a misleading impression to the public.

The company name must be displayed at the registered office and places of business as well as on company documents.

Crucial tip	There is nothing to prevent a company using a business name as well as a company name if it wants to.

Crucial concept	**Company property.** A company can own property and enter into contracts in its own name because it is a separate legal entity.

Crucial concept	**Company finances.** A company can raise capital to finance the company by issuing shares. If it wants to raise finance by way of loans, it can offer company assets as security and has the added advantage of being able to obtain a loan by way of a floating charge.

In small private companies where the company has few assets lenders will probably require a personal guarantee from the company's directors.

Crucial concept	**Company ownership and management.** A company is owned by the members but it is managed on a day-to-day basis by the directors. In small private companies owners and directors are usually the same people but in larger companies those who run the company do not necessarily own it.
	A company member's liability is limited which means that once he has paid in full for his shares he cannot be required to make any further payments to the company even if the company cannot pay its debts.

Quick test

1. What legal formalities does a sole trader have to follow if he wants to use a business name?
2. What does it mean when we say partners are jointly and severally liable?
3. What must a company do before it can start trading?

Section 4	**What happens when sole traders, partnerships and limited liability companies cease to trade?**

What are you studying?

This section describes what happens when a business organisation ceases to trade. It considers what happens when the business ceases to trade due to insolvency and how this affects the owners.

How will you be assessed on this?

Questions dealing with business cessation usually focus on what happens when a business ceases to trade because it is insolvent. It is important to recognise the differences between those who have personal liability for business debts such as sole traders and partners and the limited liability of those who trade through a limited liability company. Questions may ask you to identify the consequences of business insolvency for sole traders, partnerships and limited liability companies.

When a business decides to stop trading it may simply pay off its debts and close down. The decision to cease trading can be forced upon it if it cannot pay its debts and the outcomes for the owners can be very different depending upon whether the owner has unlimited or limited liability for the business debts.

Sole traders

If a sole trader wishes to cease trading he has two choices: he can sell his business to someone else as a going concern; or he can sell off his business assets one by one. The first course of action is preferable as he will make more money by selling the business as a going concern as he can probably sell the goodwill of the business.

> Crucial concept | **Goodwill.** Goodwill is the value placed upon the probability of former customers still using the same business even when it is taken over by someone else. It could be said that the new owner is buying the former owner's good business reputation.

If the sole trader is forced to cease trading because he is insolvent he will probably be declared bankrupt, because he has unlimited liability for his business debts.

> Crucial concept | **Bankruptcy.** A creditor who is owed more than £750 can commence bankruptcy proceedings against the debtor. If a sole trader is made bankrupt he will have to surrender all his assets, apart from domestic necessities and the tools of his trade, in order to pay his creditors. He will be unable to obtain credit for more than £250 without disclosing his bankruptcy and will be placed on a register of bankrupts until he is discharged. Bankruptcy usually lasts for three years but even after discharge it is often difficult for former bankrupts to get credit. This makes it very difficult for sole traders to restart a business.

Crucial tip	An alternative to bankruptcy is for a debtor to try to make a Voluntary Arrangement with his creditors.

Crucial concept	**Individual Voluntary Arrangement (IVA).** An IVA is a scheme set up with the approval of the court and the consent of creditors whereby the debtor agrees to make payments of agreed sums to his creditors. This scheme is supervised by an insolvency practitioner (usually an accountant or solicitor experienced in managing insolvency).

Partnerships

Crucial concept	**Partnership dissolution.** A partnership is dissolved when a partner gives notice to his fellow partners that he wishes to leave, when a partner dies, when a partner becomes bankrupt or when the agreed term for the partnership has ended.

Arrangements to continue a partnership can be made in a partnership deed, so that remaining partners can continue the partnership if they want to. Most partnership deeds will make provision for the departure of a partner and most importantly set out the financial arrangements for a partner's withdrawal.

If a partnership intends to cease trading, all the assets of the partnership will have to be sold in order to pay the firm's creditors in full. Assets remaining will be shared amongst the partners.

Crucial concept	**Partnership insolvency.** If the partnership is insolvent, all the partnership assets would have to be used to pay the partnership creditors. Individual partners would have to pay the outstanding partnership debts from their personal finances. Partnership insolvency can lead to the bankruptcy of individual partners.

Alternatively, a partnership can try to make a Voluntary Arrangement with its creditors or seek an Administration Order.

Crucial concept	**Voluntary Arrangements and Administration Orders.** A Voluntary Arrangement allows the firm to make proposals to its creditors for the settlement of its debts by a binding agreement. An Administration Order can seek to rescue the firm and with the creditors' approval put forward plans for its survival or more advantageously realise its assets if survival is not possible.

Limited liability companies

A company can be wound up by three means:

- members' voluntary winding up;
- creditors' voluntary winding up;
- compulsory winding up.

> **Crucial concepts**
>
> **Members' voluntary winding up.** A company must be able to pay its debts within one year of deciding to wind up and the directors must make a statutory declaration that the company is solvent. This method of winding up would be used where a company decides to cease trading and is not insolvent.
>
> **Creditors' voluntary winding up.** If the directors cannot make the statutory declaration as to the company's solvency or if a liquidator appointed by the members considers the company cannot meet its debts it becomes a creditors' voluntary winding up. The role of the liquidator is to get in the company's assets, realise them and pay off the creditors.
>
> **Compulsory winding up.** This usually occurs where the company cannot pay its debts and the creditors petition the court to have the company wound up.

> **Crucial tip**
>
> A debt of over £750 could trigger a company's compulsory winding up!

When a limited liability company is wound up, the members have limited liability which means that they do not have to meet the debts of the company from their personal assets.

As an alternative to an insolvent winding up a company can enter into a Company Voluntary Arrangement or an Administration Order.

> **Crucial concept**
>
> **Company Voluntary Arrangement.** This allows a company to avoid insolvency proceedings and enter into an agreed arrangement with its creditors for the settlement of its debts. For example, the creditors may agree to 50p in the £1 in full settlement of their debts.

> **Crucial concept**
>
> **Administration Order.** This is designed to achieve the survival of the company or a more effective realisation of its assets than could be achieved on a winding up.

Quick test

1. What happens to a sole trader's assets if he becomes bankrupt?
2. What is the purpose of a partnership voluntary arrangement?
3. What is the difference between a members' voluntary winding up and a creditors' voluntary winding up?

Crucial examples

1. Who bears the greatest financial risk in running a business – a sole trader or a member of a limited company? Give the reasons for your answer.

2. Define the main characteristics of operating as:
   (a) a sole trader;
   (b) a partnership;
   (c) a limited liability company.

3. Lucy and Farinda, have recently qualified as interior designers. They are thinking of setting up their own business as interior designers/decorators. They think they would like to call their business 'The Complete Room'. What advice would you give them about their choice of name?

4. Aaron and Nick want to set up business together as furniture restorers. They have £8,000 each to invest in the business. They want to avoid masses of business paperwork and they do not want to operate under complicated legal rules. Also they do not want to make their financial details public. Suggest a type of business organisation that might suit their needs. What would be the advantages and disadvantages of operating under the business organisation you have suggested?

Answers

1. You would need to discuss the concept of corporate and unincorporated bodies and identify a sole trader as an unincorporated body and a limited company as a corporate body. You would then have to identify the concept of limited and unlimited liability, pointing out that a sole trader has unlimited liability whereas a member of a limited company has limited liability. It would be a good idea to explain by reference to the case of *Salomon* v *Salomon and Co. Ltd* what limited liability means for a company member. You should explain that if a limited company becomes insolvent, a member only loses the amount he paid for his shares; if a sole trader's business fails he may become bankrupt. The consequences of becoming bankrupt should be discussed.

2. Most of the characteristics of the three types of business organisations can be found in Sections 2 and 3 of this chapter.

   The essential characteristics of a sole trader are: unlimited liability, total control, lack of formality in setting up and operating, financial privacy, stress and worry of operating alone, and difficulty in raising loans.

   The essential characteristics of the partnership are: unlimited liability (explain joint and several liability), easy to set up but offer reasons as to why it is wise to have a partnership deed, capital input by partners, shared skills and expertise and financial privacy, paid out of profits which must be shared with other partners, agency relationship between partners, the partnership does not have a separate identity from its partners.

   The essential characteristics of a limited liability company are: separate legal personality (*Salomon* v *Salomon*), can own property and make transactions in its own name, members have limited liability, raising finance is easier (shares and loans), management and ownership can be separate, companies must register with the Registrar of Companies before trading can start, companies must make annual returns to the Registrar and finances are open to public inspection.

3. Identify this as a business name and explain what this means. Explain the regulations under the Business Names Act 1985 and consider whether this name would require approval. It is unlikely that this name is offensive or requires approval. Point out that the name must be displayed on documents and premises. Remember the tort of passing off and get them to check that they are not using a name which could be confused with that of another similar business.

4. It would seem that Nick and Aaron may find that a partnership would suit their needs. Explain to them that because they do not want to do much paperwork or have to follow lots of legal rules when setting up or operating, they may not wish to become a private limited company. Setting up and operating as a partnership could avoid a good deal of this and they would not have to make any public declaration of their finances. However, they should be aware of the financial risks they will be taking. They will have unlimited liability and be each others' agents. If they do not write a partnership deed, they will be subject to the Partnership Act.

At the end of the day they will have to weigh up the financial risks of operating as a partnership against the security of a limited liability company.

Crucial reading and research

Keenan and Riches, *Business Law*, 6th edn., Longman, Chapters 5 and 6.

Holmes, Evans, Wright and Wright, *Law for Small Businesses*, 3rd edn., Pitman, Chapters 1 and 11.

CHAPTER 6

COMPANIES

Chapter summary

This Chapter considers the nature and types of companies that can exist. It explores the advantages of incorporation and the legal personality of a company. It examines how a company is set up. It looks at the financial operations, the management and the member's (shareholder's) role in the company.

Studying this Chapter will help you to:

- understand and use appropriate legal terms associated with company law;

- identify the legal requirements necessary to set up a company;

- appreciate how a company can be financed;

- explain the importance of members' meetings and members' rights;

- identify how the company is managed and the duties of directors.

Assessment targets

Target 1: explaining legal terms

You must be able to explain the legal terms used in company law. Exercise 1 at the end of this chapter will test your knowledge of these terms.

Target 2: identifying legal requirements

You must be able to explain how a company limited by shares would be set up. It may be necessary for you to know what documents are required and what they should contain. Exercise 2 at the end of this chapter will test your ability to do this.

Target 3: identifying capital

You must be able to identify the various types of capital available to a company. You will need to know the difference between share capital and loan capital. Exercise 3 at the end of this chapter will check whether you can explain the differences.

Target 4: identifying interaction in company management

You need to recognise the interaction between directors and members. Problem questions can contain a combination of issues concerning directors' duties and shareholders' rights so you must study both these topics. Exercise 4 at the end of this chapter will test your ability to identify management issues and members' responses.

Crucial terms, cases and Acts

Veil of incorporation
Companies Act 1985
Pre-incorporation contracts
Off the shelf companies
Memorandum
Articles of Association
Share capital
Loan capital
Resolutions
Voting

Rights of minority shareholders
Foss v *Harbottle* (1843)
Appointment of directors
Removal and retirement of directors
Disqualification of directors
Company Directors Disqualification Act 1986
Directors' personal liability
Powers of directors
Directors' duties

Relevant links

For a comparison with other types of business organisations and a brief overview of companies, see **Chapter 5**. See Section 4 of **Chapter 5** for winding up of companies.

| Section 1 | The nature of a company |

What are you studying?

This section identifies different types of companies and considers the idea of corporate personality.

How will you be assessed on this?

Questions may ask you to make some comparison between public and private limited companies. For this you need to know about different types of companies and be able to identify whether a company is a public or private company. You should be aware of the concept of corporate personality. Questions dealing with this concept usually ask why the corporate veil will be lifted.

Types of companies

There are a number of different types of companies; some are quite rare, for example, *chartered companies*, which are formed by grant of charter from the Crown (for example, The Institute of Chartered Accountants), and *statutory companies* which are formed by special Act of Parliament (for example, the former public utilities).

The most important type of company is the *registered company*.

REGISTERED COMPANIES

These are incorporated by registration. The relevant legislation is the *Companies Act* 1985. A company can register as:

- an unlimited company;
- a limited company which can be a public or private company.

Unlimited company

This type of company has a separate corporate personality. Its members have personal liability if the company cannot meet its debts in full in a liquidation. It does not have to file annual accounts and can maintain secrecy about its affairs.

Limited company

The liability of the company's members is limited.

Crucial tip	Limitation of liability refers to the members and not to the company itself. The company has unlimited liability to the extent of its assets.

A company limited by guarantee

Members are required to contribute a guaranteed sum if the company is unable to meet its debts. These companies are formed for charitable or educational purposes or by professional bodies.

A company limited by shares

A member's liability is limited to the amount of shares he has. A fully paid up shareholder has no further liability to the company.

Public company

Its memorandum states that it is a public company. It uses the term 'plc' after its name. It requires at least two members and two directors and a minimum subscribed share capital of £50,000 of which 25% must be paid up share capital. The company must have a secretary who is qualified within the terms of the Companies Act 1985. A company must be public if it wishes to raise capital from any source other than its founders or those introduced privately. A public company must have a trading certificate as well as its certificate of incorporation before it can begin trading.

Crucial tip	Being a public company does not mean it is automatically listed on the Stock Exchange.

Private company

A private company uses the term 'Ltd' after its name. A private company cannot offer its shares to the public. A private company needs only one director and a secretary and can operate with only one member (see overleaf).

> **Crucial tip**   An unlimited company or a company limited by guarantee must be a private company.

Single member private company
It is possible to register and operate a single member company. Minimum share capital can be £1 but the company still must have two officers – a director and a secretary.

SMALL AND MEDIUM SIZED COMPANIES
For accounting and disclosure purposes it is possible for a private company to define itself as a small or medium sized company, by reference to turnover, balance sheet total and the number of employees. This lessens the burdens upon the company in respect of the form and contents of the returns it has to make annually, for example, abbreviated balance sheets and modified profit/loss accounts. It can maintain a greater degree of confidentiality than a public company.

PARENT/HOLDING AND SUBSIDIARY COMPANIES
Companies may act as holding companies which control and usually substantially own subsidiary companies. It is common for a major public company to operate a group of companies in this way. Such relationships must be disclosed by the parent company. When preparing its accounts it must prepare and submit group accounts.

> **Crucial concept**   **Veil of incorporation.** Once a company is incorporated it is regarded as a separate legal entity. It acquires what is known as a *veil of incorporation*. This prevents its members being held responsible for the company's actions. There are a number of situations where the lifting of the corporate veil is permitted so that the human and commercial dealings behind the veil can be investigated.

> **Crucial tip**   The concept of the corporate veil was first illustrated in the case of *Salomon* v *Salomon and Co. Ltd* (1897). (See Chapter 5, Section 1.)

The veil may be lifted in the following situations:

Group situations
It may be argued that a group of companies are in reality one 'single economic entity', i.e. they are one company because they are not independent in human or commercial terms.

Agency relationship
A subsidiary company may be regarded as the agent of a holding company where both companies consent to the subsidiary acting on the holding company's behalf and under the holding company's control. The effect of establishing agency is that the actions of the subsidiary company are seen as those of the parent company.

National emergency
The veil may be drawn aside in order to establish that a company was owned by nationals of an enemy country so that to do business with it would be trading with the enemy.

Companies founded on fraud/sham or for improper purposes
The veil will be lifted where a company operation is designed to defeat the law or evade liabilities. For example, where an individual tries to hide behind a corporate front in order to evade personal obligations.

Example: Gilford Motor Co. Ltd v Horne (1933)

A former employee of Gilford Motors, who was bound by a restraint clause not to set up a rival car business and poach Gilford's customers, claimed that by setting up a company which was a separate legal entity he was not in breach of the restraint clause. The court granted Gilford Motors an injunction to stop the former employee using a company to defeat the restraint clause.

Quasi partnership companies

Where a limited company is formed out of a personal relationship based upon mutual trust and confidence it is said to be incorporated as a 'quasi partnership' company. If that relationship breaks down the courts may not merely look at the strict legal rights of a shareholder but at his legitimate expectations. For example, if a founding member director is excluded from management.

Statutory requirements

There are a number of situations where statutory requirements may demand the lifting of the veil of incorporation. These are mainly associated with tax and insolvency matters. For example:

- a public company carrying on business with less than the minimum number of members;
- establishing a holding/subsidiary company relationship where the holding company has obligations to prepare group financial accounts;
- establishing personal liability of company officers who sign company cheques without the correct company name being on the cheque;
- personal liability attributed to directors guilty of fraudulent/wrongful trading in the event of company insolvency.

A company's legal liabilities

A company is liable for its contractual commitments.

A company can be liable in tort for the actions of its employees and agents and can be liable for its employees' safety and for acts of nuisance.

A company can commit certain criminal offences in the course of its business activities. For example, giving false trade descriptions, being in breach of health and safety and environmental rules and even corporate manslaughter.

> Crucial tip   A company cannot commit a criminal act involving a physical act which an artificial legal person could not commit, for example, rape.

Quick test

1. What are the differences between a public and a private limited company?
2. Under what circumstances will the courts lift the corporate veil?

Section 2	Setting up a limited liability company

What are you studying?

This section describes the statutory procedures which must be followed in order to set up a company. The procedure for setting up a company is governed by the Companies Act 1985.

How will you be assessed on this?
It is quite common for examination questions to ask what the requirements are for setting up a limited liability company. Sometimes questions may feature more specific details and ask what the contents of a company's memorandum or its articles should contain.

Promoters

A promoter is one who undertakes to form a company, with reference to a given project, and takes the necessary steps to accomplish that purpose. It usually involves finding people to act as first directors, obtaining plant, premises and equipment.

Crucial tip	If a sole trader or partnership decides to become a limited liability company the former owners usually take on the role of promoters and become the first directors of the new company.

Crucial concept	**Pre-incorporation contracts.** A company cannot be bound by a contract made by a promoter on its behalf prior to incorporation and any attempt to do so will be ineffective. A promoter who does this will be personally liable.

Crucial tip	A company does not exist in law until it has been registered with the Registrar of Companies.

The promoter can only avoid personal liability if it has been expressly agreed that:

- the contract states that the company, when registered, will enter into the same contract and the promoter's liability will then end;

- the promoter enters into an agreement which is not legally binding.

Company registration procedure

The following information must be delivered to the Registrar of Companies together with a registration fee in order to register a limited company:

- Memorandum;

- Articles of Association;

- details of the subscribers, first directors and secretary of the company;

- address of the company's registered office;

- statutory declaration that registration requirements have been complied with by a solicitor, first director or company secretary.

Following submission of the above, the Registrar of Companies will issue a Certificate of Incorporation to a company. A private company can then begin trading, but a public company requires a trading certificate before it can commence trading. Once a certificate of incorporation has been issued, the company exists as a legal entity.

> **Crucial concept** **Off the shelf companies.** As an alternative to setting up and registering a new company it is possible to buy companies already incorporated and in existence. These companies are deliberately created for sale and have not traded prior to purchase. The advantages of buying an 'off the shelf' company are that it is quicker to set up and does not involve the purchaser in all the registration procedures.

Although it may be quicker and easier to acquire a ready made company it is usually still necessary to change the company's name, appoint suitable directors and a company secretary and bring in new shareholders.

MEMORANDUM

> **Crucial concept** **The Memorandum of a company.** When setting up a company it is essential to register a memorandum which governs the company's dealings with the world at large.

The Memorandum must contain the following details:

Name of the company

A company limited by shares must have 'limited' or 'Ltd' at the end of its name if it is a private limited company or 'plc' at the end of its name if it is a public limited company. A company cannot take a name already registered to another company or a name which has criminal or offensive connotations.

A company would need the consent of the Secretary of State for Trade and Industry for inclusion of certain words in its name which would suggest a connection with central or local government. Other sensitive names such as Royal, national or European, may require approval from government departments or other bodies.

> **Crucial tip** Before choosing a company name it is wise to check the Index of Names at Companies House and the Trade Mark Index.

A company can trade under a business name, which may be different from its company name, provided the company name appears on all company documentation and is visible outside the company's registered office and other places of business.

A company can register its Internet name and addresses through an Internet service provider provided the name has not already been allocated. The general rule is that if two users want the same Internet name the user that registered it first has the right to use it.

Registered office

The Memorandum only need state the country (England and Wales or Scotland) in which the company has its registered office. This clause cannot be altered. A company must have a registered office to which all official communications can be addressed. Official company documents must be kept here. For example, the register of members, minutes of meetings and register of directors. The address of the company's registered office must appear on all its letterheads.

The precise location of the company's registered office must be submitted to the Registrar in a statement delivered upon registration.

Objects clause

This clause must state the purpose for which the company has been formed and in theory the company can only make contracts which fall within the scope of its stated objects. Any activities beyond this would, at one time, have been '*ultra vires*' (beyond its powers) and void at common law.

When the United Kingdom entered the European Economic Community it had to comply with various company law Directives and one of these Directives, now contained within s. 35 Companies Act 1985 (as amended by the Companies Act 1989), virtually abolished the *ultra vires* rule. This means that a company can enter into any contract it wishes even if it is beyond its stated objects.

Section 35A of the 1985 Act also establishes that even where the company directors exceed the powers of the board, the company is bound by the transactions or acts they agree to on behalf of the company provided the third party who transacts with them acts in good faith. The third party has no obligation to check if the company has the capacity to carry out the transaction or act nor does he have to check upon the authority of the directors.

These changes mean that a company can sue and be sued for breaches of such obligations. However, if the transaction or act has not been concluded or legal obligations have not yet arisen, the company's shareholders can seek an injunction to prevent the company performing an *ultra vires* act or the directors exceeding their powers.

Crucial tip	These provisions do not exclude the directors from liability to the company if they cause the company loss by acting outside their powers, but it is within the company's power to grant them relief from liability.

Nowadays a company can state in its Memorandum that the object of the company is to carry on business as a general commercial company. This enables it to carry on any trade or business it chooses and gives it the power to do all such things as are incidental or conducive to such trade or business.

Limited liability clause

This clause states that the company is limited by shares unless it is an unlimited company and the clause is then omitted.

Crucial tip	If the company is a public limited company (plc) it should state this in the Memorandum.

Capital clause

This clause states what the company's nominal/authorised capital will be. This is the maximum nominal value of shares the company can issue. For example, £10,000 divided into 10,000 £1 shares.

Association clause

This clause states that the subscribers declare an intention to be associated as a company and agree to take shares.

ARTICLES OF ASSOCIATION

Crucial concept	**Articles of Association.** Articles regulate the internal management of a company and provide rules by which the company operates.

A company limited by shares either submits its own Articles or adopts a standard set of Articles known as Table A Articles. Table A can be partially adopted and modified by a company's own Articles.

Articles cannot:

- contain anything illegal;
- contain anything forbidden by company law;
- extend or modify the Memorandum;

but can:

- permit something not expressly or impliedly forbidden in the Memorandum;
- stipulate conditions upon which a member may remain a shareholder in the company.

Articles must be:

- printed;
- divided into paragraphs;
- numbered;
- signed by the subscribers.

Contents of the Articles

Articles deal with matters such as: share capital, transfer of shares, rights associated with classes of shares, conduct and voting at general meetings, appointment, powers and duties of directors, accounts and audits and dividends.

Alteration of Articles

This can be done by special resolution or consent of all the members but alterations cannot be made which prevent any further alteration of the Articles.

An alteration must not:

- conflict with the Memorandum;
- deprive members of rights given them by virtue of the Companies Acts or the courts;
- require members to take more shares or commit more capital to the company;
- amount to a fraud on the minority of shareholders.

An alteration must be made in good faith and be for the benefit of the company as a whole. This is taken to mean the bulk of the shareholders.

THE MEMBERSHIP CONTRACT

The terms of the Memorandum and Articles of Association of a company represent a contract between the company and each individual member and between the members. Failure to honour the contract obligations would be a breach of contract by the parties. Members can only enforce their rights as company members and not in any other personal capacity.

Quick test

1. What details must be included in a company's Memorandum?
2. What does *ultra vires* mean in relation to a company's objects?

Section 3 — Financing the company

What are you studying?

This section deals with the ways that a company is financed and identifies the particular features of share capital and loan capital.

How will you be assessed on this?

You may be asked straightforward questions as to your knowledge of the terminology associated with share and loan capital. You may also be asked to summarise the differences between share and loan capital.

A limited company is financed by two means:

- share capital;
- loan capital.

The Companies Acts lay down rules regarding the raising of share capital and its maintenance. Creditors have a right to see that capital is not misused and that the company does not reduce its capital in any unauthorised manner.

A company's borrowing powers are regulated by its own constitution and by the willingness of lenders to offer it loan capital.

> Crucial concept — **Share capital.** Where a company is limited by shares its capital is divided into shares. The share is the shareholders' interest in the company measured by a sum of money.

Share capital

CATEGORIES

There are different categories of share capital:

Nominal/authorised capital

This is the figure stated in the company's Memorandum. It states the number of shares that the company can issue and the nominal value of each share. A shareholder must pay the full nominal value for a share, as shares cannot be issued at a discount. However, shares are sometimes issued at a premium, that is more than the nominal value of the share. The shareholder then has to pay the nominal value plus the premium.

> Crucial tip — There is no requirement for a company to issue all its nominal capital.

Issued/allotted capital

This represents the number of shares issued to members. It is the most accurate picture of the company's worth as it represents the actual amount of shares that have been taken up by members.

Called up capital

Where a company has issued shares which are not fully paid up it can call upon the shareholders to pay the full amount at a later date. Uncalled capital is the amount remaining unpaid on shares.

Paid up capital

This represents the amount that the shareholder has paid upon his share. If the shareholder has fully paid for his shares, he has fulfilled his financial obligations to the company.

A share is a form of personal property which is transferable according to the terms of the company's Articles. It represents a member's proportionate interest in the company's business. It does not give the member ownership or control of the company's assets; it gives him a right to a share of the company's profits, in the form of a dividend. Dividends can only be paid out of company profits. Shareholders have no right to demand a dividend unless the company, through its directors, chooses to issue one. Their shares may give them a right to vote at company meetings if their class of shares have voting rights.

CLASSES OF SHARES

Companies can issue shares of different values with different rights attached to them:

Ordinary/equity shares

These shares carry voting rights at general meetings. They are seen as carrying the greatest risk but can receive the greatest returns if the company makes substantial profits.

Preference shares

These shares usually carry a right to a fixed dividend which is paid in priority to ordinary share dividends. Often the dividend is cumulative, which means that if it cannot be paid in full one year, the company must make up the difference the next year. Preference shares do not grant full voting rights in general meetings.

Redeemable shares

These shares are issued for a period after which the company can buy them back. They can be issued as preference or non-preference shares. A company can only issue these shares if it has also issued other non-redeemable shares. The issue of these shares is favoured by small companies seeking to expand and in need of short-term capital.

Deferred shares

The holders of these shares only receive a dividend after the ordinary shareholders receive a dividend. They are usually held by company founders but are not a common form of shareholding.

THE ISSUE OF SHARES

Company shares are issued by directors with the authority of the members. Members may give the directors a general authority to allot shares or a particular authority in respect of only one issue. In a public company, the directors' authority will only last for up to five years and then the members must renew it; in a private company this period can be extended indefinitely.

PRE-EMPTION RIGHTS

After the first subscription of shares, further allotments must be offered to existing members first in proportion to their shareholdings, for example, one new share for every two shares the member holds.

This pre-emption right may be excluded in the Articles of private companies or disapplied by special resolution in both public and private companies.

ACQUIRING SHARES

Following a first issue of shares a private company can only offer shares privately, whereas a public company can offer its shares to the public. A shareholder does not become a member of the company until he is placed on the register of members. Once a member, the shareholder can sell or transfer his shares. Shares in public companies are freely transferable but in private companies the Articles can restrict transfer and transfer could be at the absolute discretion of the directors.

On a first issue, a company cannot sell its shares at less than their nominal value and must only sell them for money or money's worth. A private company can give shares in return for services. For example, the services of a director.

Public companies usually issue shares to the public by means of a prospectus. This is a document which explains to the would-be investor what the company is about and what he would be getting for his investment. Preparing a prospectus is a complex business and is governed by financial services regulations which require the issue to be overseen by an authorised organisation such as a merchant bank or a broker. This organisation, known as an issuing house, acquires the shares from the company and sells them on to the public. There are civil and criminal penalties imposed upon those who issue misleading prospectuses to the public.

The Stock Exchange runs two markets for company securities. The *Listed Market* covers large public companies that are to be officially listed. These companies must comply with strict Stock Exchange listing rules. The *Alternative Investment Market* is for less prestigious public companies, where the admission rules are more relaxed.

Generally a company is not permitted to provide financial assistance to anyone wanting to purchase the company's shares, but there are exceptions to this rule and in particular private companies can offer such assistance.

Companies can issue redeemable shares and can in certain limited circumstances purchase their own shares. Public companies can only do this out of profits or from proceeds of a fresh issue but private companies can purchase them out of their capital reserves.

Loan capital

> **Crucial concept** — **Loan capital.** Apart from raising capital by way of shares, companies can borrow money to finance their business operations.

Companies usually have the power to borrow money expressly stated in their Memorandum but it is in any event an implied power given to trading companies. It is possible for a company's Articles to limit the borrowing powers of its directors. Companies borrow against their assets charging them as security for their loans. Most recognised lenders will not loan money to a company without knowing that they can recover the value of the loan if the company defaults.

> **Crucial tip** — A lender does not acquire an interest in the company but simply remains a creditor with a claim against the company.

Debentures
This is a document which acknowledges that a company has borrowed money under a secured loan. There are commonly three forms of debenture:

Single debenture
This is a loan from a single creditor, usually a bank, setting out the terms of the loan, the interest to be paid, the security offered and the terms of repayment.

Debentures issued in series
Where a company raises loans from a number of lenders, each lender contributes part of the whole sum borrowed and each lender receives a debenture which indicates that they have equal rights and security to all the other lenders.

Debenture stock
A public company may seek loans from the public. It can invite people to subscribe for debenture stock. The lender will receive a stock certificate which is similar to a share certificate. He will be able to freely transfer this on the Stock Exchange as he would shares. When a company issues debenture stock it enters into a trust deed with trustees who hold the stock on behalf of the lenders. The trustees, often insurance companies, become the creditors of the company and act on behalf of the lenders. The trustees take a charge over the company's assets and usually have wide powers given them in the deed to protect the lenders' interests.

Crucial tip	Debenture holders are not company members; they are creditors. They will receive interest, not dividend, on their loans and this can be paid out of capital. Debentures can be issued at a discount. A company can buy its own debentures.

TYPES OF CHARGES
A company may secure its borrowing by two means: a fixed charge and a floating charge.

A fixed charge
The charge attaches to specific property owned by the company at the time of its creation. Items such as land or fixed plant are most appropriate for such charges. Once a charge is made over a specific asset, the company cannot dispose of the asset without the consent of the debenture holder. If the company defaults on the loan, the debenture holder can sell the asset to recover the money owed.

Floating charge
A floating charge allows a company to raise a loan by mortgaging its assets but the charge does not attach to any specific asset as it does with a fixed charge. The charge would only crystallise upon specific company assets in the event of the company defaulting upon the loan or under circumstance specified in the charge. A floating charge usually relates to a company's changing assets such as its stock in trade, its goodwill or its book debts. A floating charge allows the company to deal with its property without having to seek the debenture holder's permission whilst it trades solvently.

Crucial tip	A debenture holder of a fixed charge is better protected in the event of a company's insolvency than a holder of a floating charge. The fixed charge holder will take priority over the holder of a floating charge.

REGISTRATION OF CHARGES

Fixed and floating charges have to be registered with the Registrar of Companies within 21 days of their creation. If a charge is not registered within that time it is void, which means that the lender would have no security over the property which the company had charged to secure the loan. The lender would become an unsecured creditor of the company in the event of the company being wound up/insolvent. Apart from registration being a protection for the lender, it shows those subsequently dealing with the company the extent of the company's borrowings. Charges take priority according to the date of their creation but a fixed charge almost always takes priority over a floating charge no matter when it was created.

Companies are required to maintain a register of all charges on their property which must be available for inspection by members and creditors.

Quick test

1. What is the difference between loan capital and share capital?
2. What classes of shares can a company issue?
3. What is the difference between a fixed charge and a floating charge?

Section 4	Members and meetings

What are you studying?

This section deals with membership meetings. It deals with the role of the member within the company and his opportunity to influence the way the company is run. It considers the member's statutory and common law rights.

How will you be assessed on this?

It is useful to know about members' meetings, how they are called and how they are run. Students should learn about members' voting rights at these meetings. Students may be asked to explain how meetings are called and conducted and the different types of resolutions that may be passed. Another favourite question area concerning members is the protection and enforcement of members' rights. This would require knowledge of the rule in *Foss* v *Harbottle* (1843) and the use of s. 459 of the Companies Act 1985.

A company member

A company member is one whose name is on the register of members.

Every company must keep a register of members containing the names, addresses and shareholding of each member at the company's registered office.

Members have very little input and influence over the day-to-day running of their company. They are statutorily entitled to certain information and rights, such as details of annual accounts and the right to attend the company's Annual General Meeting (AGM). There are certain aspects of company business that have to be voted on by the members, such as major changes to the company's constitution.

To an extent, a company member's influence over the company's business can be measured by their voting power. Those who control the majority of shares can exercise the greatest influence.

Types of meetings

Members' meetings are usually called by the directors. All members can attend and speak but not all members can vote on resolutions. A member needs shares carrying voting rights to do this.

ANNUAL GENERAL MEETING (AGM)

An AGM must be held once per year. Members are entitled to 21 days' notice in writing. The purpose of an AGM is to discuss the company's financial position, question directors as to management reports, review annual accounts and reports, appoint and reappoint directors and auditors.

If the directors default in holding an AGM the Department of Trade and Industry may call a meeting on the application of a member.

EXTRAORDINARY GENERAL MEETINGS (EGM)

Any members' meeting other than an AGM is classed as an EGM. Fourteen days' notice is required to convene an EGM. EGM's are called for matters that require immediate attention and cannot wait until the next AGM or where statute requires that the directors call a meeting, for example, if the company has suffered a serious reduction in its capital.

CLASS MEETINGS

These may be held by a particular class of shareholders, for example, preference shareholders and may decide matters relating to that particular class of shares.

Calling a meeting

Directors usually call a members' meeting, issue agenda and statements relating to the matters to be discussed but members can requisition a meeting if necessary. It usually requires two or more members holding one-tenth of the voting paid up share capital to call a members' meeting.

POWER OF COURT TO ORDER MEETINGS

If a meeting cannot be properly called or constituted in a manner prescribed by the company the courts have power to convene a meeting at their own motion or at the request of a director or voting member.

NOTICE OF MEETINGS

Notice of meetings must be sent to all members, directors and company auditors. The length of notice required is dependent upon the nature of the issues under discussion and the type of meeting. The notice must state the place, time and nature of the business to be discussed and the member's proxy rights.

A meeting can be called at short notice: for an AGM all the members must agree; for any other meeting 95% of members must agree. This can be reduced to 90% for private companies.

Resolutions

Crucial concept   A **resolution** is an expression of opinion or intention, by a meeting.

Resolutions passed at meetings may be invalid if:

- not all the members have been informed of the meeting;

- the meeting is not quorate.

(Quorate means that a stated minimum number of people must be present to allow the business to be transacted.)

Resolutions of the members of a company are either special, extraordinary or ordinary.

SPECIAL RESOLUTION

A special resolution requires 21 days' notice and a 75% majority of votes cast of members present and voting. This type of resolution would be used to change the company name or alter the company's Articles.

EXTRAORDINARY RESOLUTION

An extraordinary resolution requires 14 days' notice and a 75% majority of votes cast. It would be used for voluntary liquidation of a company or a class meeting of shareholders to alter or vary class rights.

ORDINARY RESOLUTION

An ordinary resolution requires a simple majority of members' votes (51%). It can be used for the removal of a director before his period of office has expired but *Special Notice* has to be given to do this. Special notice requires 28 days' notice to the company and 21 days' notice to members. Special notice is used for:

- removal of directors;

- appointment/reappointment of plc directors over the age of 70;

- removal of an auditor.

> **Crucial tip**   When a specified majority of members are required to pass a resolution it does not mean a majority of the members of the company but only those entitled to vote and who attend and vote (or vote by proxy).

WRITTEN RESOLUTION

This is a resolution agreed upon and signed by all the members of a private company. It can be passed without the need to call a meeting. It cannot be used for the removal of directors or auditors.

ELECTIVE RESOLUTION

This resolution needs the unanimous consent of all the members and 21 days' notice is required of the meeting at which it is to be proposed. These resolutions are only available to private companies. They are used for giving directors authority to allot shares, dispensing with the laying of accounts and reports before general meetings, dispensing with AGM's, dispensing with the annual appointment of auditors and reduction of the majority required to authorise short notice of meetings.

An elective resolution can be passed by a written resolution. It can be revoked at any general meeting by the passing of an ordinary resolution.

Copies of special, extraordinary and elective resolutions must be sent to the registrar of companies within 15 days of their being passed.

MINUTES OF MEETINGS

These must be written up, signed and kept as a true record. Members may inspect these. Copies of written resolutions must also be recorded and kept.

Voting

> **Crucial concept**   **Voting.** A member's right to vote is a property right so he can vote whatever way he wants to and for whatever motive he chooses. Members entitled to vote can vote on a show of hands or on a poll.

POLL

A poll usually gives one vote per share. A company cannot exclude member's rights to demand a poll if five voting members or those with 10% of voting rights so demand. Upon a poll, a proxy (see below) has the same rights as the member he represents.

> **Crucial tip** A poll may be demanded as a fairer way of reflecting shareholders' wishes because voting on a show of hands means each member has one vote regardless of the number of shares they hold.

PROXIES

A proxy can attend a meeting in place of a member, who may direct the proxy as to how he should vote on a poll. The company must be informed if a proxy is to be used. Proxies cannot vote on a show of hands.

Protecting the rights of shareholders

The principle of majority control is clearly recognised in companies. The shareholders holding the majority of the votes can wield considerable influence. They can control appointments to the Board of Directors and equally can dismiss directors if they think the company is being run oppressively or unfairly. Minority shareholders do not have such advantages; they cannot challenge unfairness in the same way and therefore need common law and statutory protection to uphold their rights. These problems are often exacerbated in small private companies where the directors are also the majority shareholders.

> **Crucial concept** **Rights of minority shareholders.** In a company majority decisions prevail and if a wrong is committed against the company the proper claimant would be the company itself. Therefore where a minority of shareholders wish to litigate against the wishes of the majority of shareholders an action would be futile. Generally the courts will not entertain an action brought by minority shareholders on behalf of the company. This principle is known as the rule in *Foss v Harbottle* (1843).

In *Foss v Harbottle*, individual shareholders were ruled to be incompetent to bring an action against the company directors who were alleged to have misapplied company property. The proper claimant was the company and as the majority of shareholders did not wish to instigate such an action the minority had no legal standing to do so.

However, there are exceptions to this rule which would allow a member to take action:

- where the company intends to commit an *ultra vires* act – the shareholder may seek an injunction to prevent the company so acting;

- an act needs a special or extraordinary resolution and therefore requires more than simple majority approval;

- a fraud has been committed on the minority and the wrongdoers are themselves in control of the company. Fraud in this context can be some sort of improper behaviour by the majority which amounts to an abuse of their power. For example, where controlling directors use their powers for improper purposes or misappropriate company assets.

> **Crucial tip** Fraud can never be ratified, even by a majority of members.

The rule in *Foss v Harbottle* does not apply where personal rights of shareholders are infringed as this would not be a wrong committed against the company.

TYPES OF ACTIONS AVAILABLE TO SHAREHOLDERS

There are a variety of actions which an individual or a group of minority shareholders can take against majority shareholders, the company or the directors.

Personal action

The shareholder would sue in his own name to enforce his own personal rights. For example, where the individual was denied his voting rights.

Representative action

Where the same personal rights of a group of shareholders have been infringed, one shareholder takes action on behalf of the group.

The relief requested in the above type of actions will be a declaratory judgment, which will state what the law is and what the parties will abide by or an injunction to restrain the conduct of a majority who have acted unfairly.

Derivative action

Where the alleged wrongdoers are in control of the company and will not permit a claim to be brought in the name of the company, the action is brought by the wronged shareholder on behalf of the company to enforce the company's rights. In this type of action the company would benefit from the proceedings and not the shareholders taking the action. The remedy of damages may be awarded.

Crucial tip	**Derivative action.** The derivative action is the usual form of action taken by shareholders who consider there has been a fraud on the minority which falls under the exception to the rule in *Foss* v *Harbottle*.

Statutory protection

By far the most popular shareholder remedy used today is the statutory remedy provided by s. 459 of the Companies Act 1985. This is referred to as the right not to be unfairly prejudiced.

Other examples of members' statutory rights are the right to object to changes in the company's objects, the right to have an item put on the agenda for an AGM and the right to ask for an EGM.

RIGHT NOT TO BE UNFAIRLY PREJUDICED

A member of the company must show that the company's affairs are being or have been conducted in a manner which is unfairly prejudicial to the interests of its members generally or some of its members, including at least himself.

Crucial tip	It is the petitioner's interests, as a company member, that must have been unfairly prejudiced.

It is up to the court to decide upon the facts of each case whether there has been unfairly prejudicial behaviour. Examples of circumstances which have been considered unfairly prejudicial are:

- excluding a member from management in a small private company where there was an expectation of such a role and the other directors/members vote the excluded member off the board;

- failure to lay accounts before members;

- failure to provide adequate advice and information to members before an acceptance of a takeover bid;

- directors paying themselves unjustifiably high salaries and failing to pay members proper dividends;

- using the company's assets for the benefit of the company's controlling shareholders and their family.

> **Crucial tip** The courts are somewhat reluctant to order a remedy under s. 459 for what a member may consider to be unfair prejudice caused by company mismanagement, poor commercial decision taking, dispute over company policy or management arrangements. Where there is evidence of a director's breach of fiduciary duties (i.e. to act in good faith) or his falling short of the expected level of care and skill then s. 459 may operate.

Relief can be granted as the court thinks fit. In deciding whether an act is unfairly prejudicial the court will take into account such facts as:

- the petitioner's conduct;
- prior knowledge of the matters complained of;
- offers made to buy out the petitioner;
- motive of the oppressor;
- delay in petitioning.

The court may order:

- future regulation of the company's affairs;
- require the company to refrain from a future course of conduct;
- authorise proceedings in the name of the company;
- purchase of a petitioner's shares at a fair value.

The court may order that the company be wound up on the grounds that it is just and equitable to do so. Members can apply to the court for this remedy in the event of management deadlock, lack of confidence in the company's management, exclusion from management or failure of company objects. This remedy is considered a remedy of last resort and should only be used if there is no alternative.

Unfair prejudice does not have to be proved to pursue this remedy but the courts encourage aggrieved members to use s. 459 wherever possible so as to avoid having to wind up the company.

In 1998 the Law Commission produced a report (No. 246), which deals with shareholder remedies. The report recommended that shareholder remedies needed to be cheaper and easier to access. It suggested that small private companies should consider inserting a dispute resolution clause in their Articles to allow dissatisfied shareholders an opportunity to leave the company in an agreed manner without needing to resort to litigation.

It also considered that derivative actions (see exceptions to *Foss v Harbottle*) were too complex and should be simplified by clear court rules.

Quick check

1. What differences are there between an AGM and an EGM?
2. What types of resolutions can be passed by members?
3. What is the fraud exception to the rule in *Foss v Harbottle*?
4. What orders can a court make where a petitioner is successful in a s. 459 action?

What are you studying?

This section deals with how the company is managed and who manages it. It considers the role of the directors. It examines their capacity to manage, their authority to manage and their duties, both at common law and under statute. It also looks at the role of the company secretary and the company's auditors.

How will you be assessed on this?

Company management and the role of directors is an important area in company law and it can feature in a number of questions that do not necessarily deal exclusively with directors. For instance members' rights may have to be considered in relation to actions that a director may take. It may be useful to know how directors are appointed and removed as members can play a part in these actions. Knowing why directors are disqualified and considered unfit to act as directors is something you should be aware of too. A question concerning the authority of the board or an individual director may also be linked with a company's capacity to contract.

A popular area for examination questions is the duties of directors. Questions can appear in problem format or may take the form of an essay where you are asked to describe the duties of directors. For these questions you need to know the common law and the statutory duties of directors.

Directors

Directors attend board meetings as of right and take part in company decision making.

Although a company is a separate legal entity, it requires management and day-to-day direction by human beings. The company directors, collectively known as the Board, fulfil this function and act as agents of the company. They control the policies that the company follows. Therefore it is essential that there are statutory as well as common law rules governing their activities, as well as internal company regulations.

APPOINTMENT

Crucial concept **Appointment of directors.** The first directors are named in the registration documents. Thereafter they are appointed by ordinary resolution in general meeting, in accordance with the Articles. Casual vacancies may be filled by appointment of the Board.

The company's Articles may regulate a director's tenure of office and may specify how directors should be appointed, replaced and removed.

The name, nationality, occupation and address of a director must be placed on a register of directors at the company's offices.

QUALIFICATIONS

No formal qualifications are required but some companies may specify certain requirements such as share qualification or age qualifications.

A director cannot be:

- an undischarged bankrupt;

- a person disqualified by the court from being a director;

- a sole director and secretary of a company.

REMOVAL AND RETIREMENT

> **Crucial concept** — **Removal and retirement of directors.** Reasons for removing a director may be stated in the company's Articles. For example, mental illness, permanent physical incapacity or age. Directors can retire or resign in accordance with the provisions in the company's Articles.

Members can remove a director by ordinary resolution. Some companies provide directors with weighted voting in the event of a threatened removal. For example, for every share the director possesses he is given three votes.

> **Crucial tip** — Removal of an executive director (see page 113) may lead to a claim for compensation if there is a breach of his service contract.

DISQUALIFICATION

> **Crucial concept** — **Disqualification of directors.** The Company Directors Disqualification Act 1986 is designed to protect the public from directors' misconduct and unfitness to act as directors.

A court can disqualify a person from being a director, promoter or becoming involved directly or indirectly with the management of a company or becoming an administrator, receiver or liquidator for the following reasons:

- conviction for an indictable offence connected with formation, management or liquidation of a company;
- persistent default in filing or making returns to the registrar of companies;
- breach of duty towards the company or fraud in the course of a winding up.

The court *must* disqualify someone who is or has been a director of a company, which has become insolvent and that person's conduct makes him unfit to be concerned in the management of a company.

Matters which are considered relevant for determining unfitness are:

- breach of duty;
- misapplication of funds;
- misfeasance (i.e. improper performance of a lawful act);
- failure to comply with requirements concerning submission of annual returns to the Registrar of Companies.
- the extent to which the director is responsible for causing the insolvency of the company;
- failure to co-operate with the liquidator in the event of a company's insolvency.

Disqualification can be from 2 to 15 years depending upon the seriousness of the director's conduct.

The Secretary of State keeps a register of disqualification orders, which is open to inspection.

> **Crucial tip**   Anyone who acts whilst disqualified commits a criminal offence. A person so acting can be jointly/severally liable with the company for managing a company whilst disqualified.

PERSONAL LIABILITY

> **Crucial concept**   **Directors' personal liability.** Where a director is liable for wrongful or fraudulent trading or misfeasance he can incur personal liability, as well as being subject to disqualification proceedings.

Wrongful trading occurs when a director negligently continues trading when he ought to have realised that the company could not avoid going into liquidation. *Fraudulent trading* is only applicable where there is evidence of actual deceit. For example, where a director clearly intended to defraud the company's creditors.

Misfeasance proceedings could occur where upon the liquidation of a company a director has misappropriated money or property belonging to the company or its creditors in breach of his fiduciary duties.

In these circumstances the court can order repayment or restoration of company money or property or require a director to contribute to the company's assets.

TYPES OF DIRECTORS
Shadow director
A shadow director is a person who is not held out or officially recognised as a director of a company but who is in a position to dictate to the actual company directors how to vote and decide policy at board meetings.

Alternate director
A person who is appointed by a director to act in his place if he is unable to attend board meetings.

Executive director
A director who holds a management position and is usually under a service contract to the company. An executive director is involved in the day-to-day management of the company.

> **Crucial tip**   Sometimes executive directors are known as working directors because they work full-time for the company.

Non-executive director
A person who attends board meetings but is not in a management position. Such directors may be paid a fee for their work but would not be under a contract of service. They are appointed because of the specialist skills or expertise they possess. The Stock Exchange Combined Code which adopted many of the recommendations of earlier reports on good management and financial responsibility in public companies suggested that listed companies should have a majority of non-executive directors on their board who would act as independent voices.

> **Crucial tip**   A company has no obligation to appoint a managing director.

Company secretary

A company must have a secretary and details of the appointment must be kept by the company. The secretary need not have specific qualifications but the secretary of a public company must have recognised professional qualifications or proven skill and experience for the job. His responsibilities include keeping all the company registers up-to-date, keeping minutes of meetings and supervising submission of the company's annual returns to the Registrar of Companies. The secretary of a listed public company also has to ensure that the company has complied with the Stock Exchange Code of Best Practice.

The secretary has power to make contracts on behalf of the company. If those contracts seem incidental to his job, for example contracts associated with the running of the company's offices, even if the secretary had no authority the company will be bound by the contract if the a third party acting in good faith believed the secretary had been authorised to make them.

Crucial tip	The secretary of a company does not have to be a director but often is a named director.

Auditors

Every active company must have auditors. Initially they are appointed by the directors and in private companies are re-elected each year by the members.

Crucial tip	Dormant and small private companies can be exempted from the requirement to hold an annual audit.

Auditors must be independent of the company and suitably qualified, for example a chartered accountant. Their job is to audit the company's accounts. To do this they should check stock, advise the company of unsatisfactory practices, verify the accuracy of the accounts and the entries therein. They should make checks to see if the accounts are hiding any errors or dishonesty. They must report to the shareholders whether the accounts give a fair picture of the company's financial affairs.

Auditors have the power to investigate the company's books and records and question company officials. They can be liable in contract if they fail to properly complete their undertaking to the company. In tort they can be liable in negligence to their client or to third parties for negligent misstatements (see Chapter 4).

The board of directors

The board's powers are collective but delegation to individual directors or a committee of directors is possible. The Stock Exchange Combined Code suggests that the board should meet regularly, retain full and effective control over the company and monitor executive management to prevent any one director having unfettered powers. General management powers are conferred on the board.

Proceedings in meetings are informal and matters are dealt with by discussion unless a vote is called for. Majority decisions are usual. Each director is entitled to attend and speak at meetings. Minutes of each meeting must be recorded and kept.

Directors as employees

Executive directors are usually employees of the company and work under fixed-term service contracts. Shareholders must approve these service contracts if they are for five years or more and cannot be terminated by notice or only in specified circumstances. Service contracts must be available for members' inspection.

Remuneration can be set by the shareholders in general meeting but often the function is delegated to the board. The Stock Exchange Combined Code recommends that remuneration committees should establish a formal and transparent procedure for developing policy on executive remuneration and on fixing individual remuneration packages.

Companies are under a duty to disclose directors' salaries in their accounts. The 'Combined Code' advises that in public limited companies, directors' individual remuneration packages and remuneration policy should be included in the company's annual report.

Directors' capacity and authority

It is advisable to consider this section in conjunction with the details on company objects contained in section 2 on the contents of the company's Memorandum.

POWERS

> **Crucial concept** **Powers of directors.** The Articles of most companies provide that the business of the company is to be managed by the directors and that they may exercise all the powers of the company. Directors should not authorise any transactions which the company's objects do not permit. Therefore directors should only use their powers for proper purposes.

It is generally considered that in the following circumstances the company would still be bound by acts agreed to by directors even where they had exceeded their authority:

Section 35A of the Companies Act 1985

Where a third party deals with the company directors in good faith, that party is not subject to any limitations or restrictions on the power of the board of directors under the company's constitution. The constitution of the company includes its Memorandum, Articles and resolutions passed in general meetings.

Law of agency

Where a director has no actual authority to enter into a transaction on behalf of the company, he may still bind the company to the transaction if it would seem reasonable to a third party to assume it would be within his usual competence. Where the board of directors have done nothing to indicate to the third party that the director has no such authority it may be said that the director has the appearance of authority and can act in that way.

The rule in *Turquand's* case (also known as the indoor management rule)

In *Royal British Bank* v *Turquand* the directors of a company exceeded their borrowing powers, as their power to borrow was subject to the passing of an ordinary resolution and no such resolution had been passed. The bank which had lent the company money on the strength of the directors' request demanded repayment of the loan from the company. The company alleged that it was not responsible for the repayment of the debt, as the directors had no authority to obtain this loan without the appropriate resolution. The company was held responsible for the debt incurred by the directors. As the bank was an outsider to the company's affairs it had no means of knowing that the appropriate resolution had not been passed.

A company's failure to follow its own rules should not penalise an innocent third party.

> **Crucial tip** Section 35A of the Companies Act 1985 has largely superseded the need for the rule in *Turquand's case*.

Directors' duties

> Crucial concept
>
> **Directors' duties.** Directors owe common law duties to the company in the form of fiduciary duties and the duty of care. They also owe a number of statutory duties which have been imposed by the Companies Acts.

Directors owe duties to the following:

Duty to the company

The directors foremost duty is owed to the company as a whole. This is taken to mean the shareholders as a collective body.

Duties to employees

Directors must have regard to the interests of the company's employees. The duty is owed through the company and therefore the employees cannot enforce it personally.

Duties to creditors

Although there is no direct duty to creditors, directors have to consider creditors' interests, especially where the company is insolvent. Failure to do so may result in the director becoming personally liable.

COMMON LAW DUTIES

Duty of care and skill

Generally the level of competence expected of a director for negligence purposes is low. Until recent years the view was of a non-qualified, non-professional who would bring no particular skills to the office of director. Provided he acted honestly and in the best interests of the company this was sufficient.

The level of care and skill expected was stated in the case of *Re City Equitable Fire Insurance Co. Ltd.* (1925):

- A director need not exhibit in the performance of his duties a greater degree of skill than may reasonably be expected from a person of his knowledge and experience. This could mean that the expectations of an unqualified, unskilled director were very low. However, if a director did have some specialist skills, it was expected that he would exercise them for the benefit of the company. Nowadays higher standards of competence are expected of those with relevant professional qualifications.

- A director is not bound to give continuous attention to the affairs of the company. His duties are of an intermittent nature to be performed at periodical board meetings. This may be an acceptable position for a non-executive director but would be wholly unacceptable for an executive director working as a full-time employee.

- Directors may delegate duties to properly qualified company employees. This would not be a breach of duty by a director and is acceptable business practice.

Where a director has breached his duty of care and skill, the company may begin an action in negligence. A director found liable may have to personally reimburse the company for its losses.

> Crucial tip
>
> There is nothing in the Companies Acts that sets out a specific standard of care and skill expected of a director.

FIDUCIARY DUTIES

To act *bona fide* and in the best interests of the company

For example, directors are expected not to place themselves in a position whereby they have a conflict between their loyalty to their company and to a third party.

To use powers for proper purposes

Directors are required to use their powers for the purposes for which they were conferred. For example, if directors have power to issue shares they must do so for the purpose of raising capital for the company and not for any ulterior motive such as favouring one group of investors over another.

Not to create a conflict of duty and interest

A company contract that a director has a personal interest in and has not been declared to the company in a general meeting can become voidable at the option of the company.

Statutorily directors are required to declare direct and indirect interests in a contract with the company to a full a board meeting. Directors can be fined for a failure to comply.

Often Articles of private companies permit a director making a disclosure to retain an interest in such contracts and keep the profits therefrom. Usually the director takes no part in the discussion or voting on such an item.

Not to make a personal gain from office

A director, who makes any unauthorised profit from his office, without disclosure, even if the company does not suffer loss, is in breach of this duty. A director is liable to account for profits made from an opportunity, which it was his duty to obtain for his company and which he exploits for his own benefit. For example, a director cannot use information that he obtains whilst in his position as company director and use it for his own benefit.

A director would be accountable for secret personal commission or bribes he received from a third party.

Where a director has committed a breach of fiduciary duty the company could apply for the director to account for the profit he made or loss which the company has sustained. A company can pass an ordinary resolution to excuse the breach, except where fraud on the minority is committed.

STATUTORY DUTIES AND OBLIGATIONS

Substantial property transactions

Where contracts involve directors or 'connected persons' transferring substantial non-cash assets, defined as property exceeding £100,000 or more than 10% of the company's net assets, whichever is the lower, to or from the company, the shareholders in a general meeting must give prior approval. It does not apply to non-cash assets of less than £2,000. Connected persons include a director's spouse, his business partners, or a company in which he has over 20% of the voting shares. Failure to observe these provisions can render a contract voidable and the director may have to account for any personal gain or company loss.

Contracts for loans and guarantees

There are statutory rules, which regulate a company's ability to make loans, give guarantees or indemnities to directors or connected persons. The rules are quite strict where 'relevant companies' (i.e. public companies) are involved but less so for private companies. Breach of these rules can render a transaction voidable at the company's option. Directors who made gains by such transactions must account for their gains and will be liable for any loss the company incurs by reason of the breach. Criminal sanction may apply in the case of 'relevant companies'.

Dealing in securities

It is a director's duty to disclose any interests he may have in his company's shares, debentures or dealings. This rule is of importance in respect of listed companies.

DIRECTORS' RELIEF FROM LIABILITY

Companies cannot exempt company officers from liabilities to the company but they can take out insurance against such personal liabilities for directors. Companies may also indemnify officers against costs incurred in defending proceedings in which judgment is given in their favour.

A court may relieve an officer of a company from liability if the court is satisfied he acted honestly, reasonably and ought to be fairly relieved of his liabilities.

Quick test

1. How may a director be removed from office?
2. What are the different types of directors?
3. List a director's fiduciary duties?

Crucial examples

1. Explain the meaning of the following terms:
   (a) veil of incorporation;
   (b) promoter;
   (c) 'off the shelf'company;
   (d) preference share;
   (e) floating charge;
   (f) special resolution;
   (g) non-executive director;
   (h) wrongful trading.

2. Describe the nature and contents of the documents that must be submitted to the Registrar of Companies before a company can be incorporated.

3. Compare and contrast equity shares and debentures as alternative forms of investment.

4. Richard, Judy and Mike are all shareholders in a company known as Marvellous Marquees Ltd. The company makes and supplies marquees for outdoor events and functions. They are all directors of the company. Richard and Judy have 30 ordinary shares each and Mike has 40 ordinary shares.

   Ted, who has developed a new lightweight waterproof material which he thinks will be ideal for tent making, approaches Mike and asks him if he is interested in trying out the material on some new marquees. Mike does not tell Richard and Judy about this opportunity but suggests to Ted that they should set up their own company to manufacture lightweight tents made out of the new material.

   Richard and Judy discover that Mike has been working secretly with Ted on this project and that he has formed a new company with Ted to manufacture and sell the lightweight tents.

   What action can they take against Mike and explain why they may take such action?

Answers

1. (a) A veil of incorporation identifies a company as a separate legal entity and draws a veil between the members and the company so that the actions of the company cannot be

attributed to the members.

Refer to *Salomon* v *Salomon and Co. Ltd* (1897).

(b) A promoter is a person who undertakes to form a company. He may obtain capital for the company, find directors and seek premises and equipment as well as submitting the company's registration documents. Promoters will be personally liable for pre-incorporation contracts.

(c) An 'off the shelf' company is a company which can be bought, that has already been incorporated and is ready to trade.

(d) A preference share is a share carrying a fixed dividend, which may be cumulative. Dividend is paid in priority to ordinary shares. A preference share does not carry voting rights.

(e) A floating charge is a charge (debt) created over the whole of the company's assets and undertakings but does not settle on any particular assets unless the charge crystallises, which would occur when the company defaulted on the charge or became insolvent. A floating charge allows a solvent company to deal with its assets and undertakings without reference to the holder of the charge.

(f) A special resolution is a members' resolution that requires 75% majority of votes cast and 21 days' notice. It is used for altering the Articles or varying class rights.

(g) A non-executive director is a director of a company who is not under a contract of service or in a management position. He attends board meetings and is appointed to the board because of his specialist skills or expert knowledge. Public companies must have a majority of non-executive directors on their boards.

(h) Personal liability may fall upon a director where he continues to trade when he ought to have realised that the company could not avoid going into insolvent liquidation. He may also be disqualified from acting as a director following a finding of wrongful trading.

2. Documents which must be submitted to the Registrar of Companies are:

- Memorandum containing details of the company's name, its registered office, its objects and associated powers, a limited liability clause, a capital clause and an association clause;
- Articles which contain details of the company's internal management arrangement, for example conduct of members meetings, appointment of directors and share transfer rules;
- details of first shareholders, first directors, first secretary and address of the company's registered office;
- a statutory declaration stating that the registration requirements have been met.

  These documents must be submitted to the Registrar of Companies together with a fee and the company should get a certificate of incorporation which will allow it to begin trading. A public company needs a trading certificate too before it can commence trading.

3. A person holding equity shares (ordinary shares) is a member of the company. Equity shares carry voting rights and entitle the holder to a share in the company's profits by way of a dividend, but only if the directors declare a dividend. They cannot be issued at a discount and they may be issued at a premium. They are the member's property and are transferable, although this may be restricted in private companies. They carry the greatest risk if the company becomes insolvent as they would lose their value and the holder would not get their capital back.

   A debenture is a document acknowledging a company's borrowing. The debenture holder is a creditor of the company and has no voting rights or ownership in the company. Debenture holders get paid an agreed rate of interest on their loan and can be paid out of the company's capital if necessary. Debentures can be issued at a discount and a company can buy its own debentures.

Debentures can be secured by a fixed or floating charge and these charges should be registered with the Registrar of Companies within 21 days of the charge being created.

4. Mike has breached his fiduciary duties as a director in Marvellous Marquees Ltd. He has not acted in the best interests of the company because he has put himself into a position where his own personal interests conflict with those of the company. As a director he had power to make contracts on behalf of the company and could have entered into a contract with Ted on behalf of the company to manufacture tents made out of this new material but he did not do so. He has used his position as a director to exploit an opportunity that should have gone to the company. He is likely to make a personal profit from the sales of these tents.

As it is the company that has suffered this lost opportunity by reason of his actions, it can initiate action against Mike. It may apply for him to account for profits he makes or losses that it has sustained.

Richard and Judy as members of the company with over 50% of the voting shares may call a members' meeting and pass an ordinary resolution under the special notice procedure to remove Mike as a director.

Unless there is something in the company's Articles which prevents members having an interest in a rival business it is unlikely that Richard and Judy can ask Mike to give up his company membership. As they do not have the necessary shareholding to change the Articles by special resolution they cannot insert such a clause.

If you are really thinking hard about this question you may go on to say that as it is a small private company where all the members play an active part in management, Mike may try to have the company wound up at this point on the grounds that it is just and equitable, as there is clearly a breakdown in management and a loss of trust and confidence. If possible Richard and Judy may try to buy out Mike's shares to prevent him destroying the company.

Crucial reading and research

Bourne, *Principles of Company Law*, 3rd edn., Cavendish.
Kelly and Holmes, *Business Law*, 3rd edn., Cavendish, Chapter 13.
Smith and Keenan, *Company Law for Students* 11th edn., Pitman.

CHAPTER 7

EMPLOYMENT
LAW

Chapter summary

This chapter gives an overview of the law of employment. It identifies how an employee differs from an independent contractor. It describes the formation and the contents of the contract of employment and identifies the duties of employers and employees with regard to the contract. In addition, it describes the ways in which the contract may come to an end. Discrimination in employment and equal pay are also considered.

Studying this chapter will help you to:

- understand the difference between an employee and an independent contractor and how the courts differentiate between them;

- identify how a contract of employment is formed and the type of terms that the contract contains;

- understand the ways in which a contract of employment may come to an end;

- understand the main sources of law on discrimination in employment and the law relating to equal pay.

Assessment targets

Target 1: identifying the difference between an employee and an independent contractor

You must know the difference between an employee and an independent contractor. You must also know when an employer is vicariously liable for the negligent acts of his workers. Exercise 1 at the end of this chapter will check whether you can do this.

Target 2: understanding terms in the contract of employment

You must know how the different types of terms are included within the contract of employment. Exercise 2 at the end of this chapter will check whether you can do this.

Target 3: identifying when a contract of employment comes to an end

You must know how a contract of employment may come to an end and when an employee may have a claim for wrongful or unfair dismissal. Exercise 3 at the end of this chapter will check whether you can do this.

Target 4: understanding discrimination and equal pay

You must understand the law relating to discrimination and equal pay. Exercise 4 at the end of this chapter will check whether you can do this.

Crucial terms, cases and Acts

Employees and independent contractors
Vicarious liability
Contract of employment
Wrongful dismissal
Unfair dismissal
Redundancy

Transfer of undertakings
Sexual discrimination
Racial discrimination
Disability discrimination
Equal pay

Relevant links

The difference between express and implied terms is explained in **Chapter 2**. Tribunals are discussed in **Chapter 1**. The tort of negligence is explained in more detail in **Chapter 4**.

Section 1	Employees and independent contractors

What are you studying?

This section outlines the differences between an employee and an independent contractor and describes the tests that the courts have used to distinguish between them. Vicarious liability is explained.

How will you be assessed on this?

You will need to know how an employee differs from an independent contractor. You must also know when an employer will be vicariously liable for the negligent acts of his workers.

Crucial concept · **Employees and independent contractors.** In basic terms an employee is employed by the employer and works under a contract of service. An independent contractor is self-employed and works under a contract for service.

It may be more financially worthwhile for a person to work as an independent contractor as he may be able to negotiate a better rate of pay and he will have certain tax advantages. However, he will receive few other benefits as much of the legislation which gives employment protection to workers, such as protection from unfair dismissal, only applies to employees.

It is often difficult to distinguish an employee from an independent contractor and so over the years the courts have developed a number of tests in an attempt to clarify the difference.

The control test
The more control that an employer has over a worker the more likely it is that the worker is an employee. This test was developed in the nineteenth century and is no longer used on its own but is used in conjunction with the other tests.

The integration test
The more a person is integrated into the workplace, the more likely it is that the person is an employee. There have been problems in applying this test. For example, some employees and independent contractors may be doing exactly the same work and it may be difficult to say who is more integrated.

The economic reality test
This test provides a more modern approach. Instead of applying a single test, a number of factors are considered. First, does this person take the financial risks and provide his own equipment? Secondly, how much control is exercised over him and is his contract consistent with a contract of employment? The court would consider such matters as who pays his tax and whether he receives sick pay and holiday pay.

> **Crucial concept** **Vicarious liability** means being responsible for the actions of someone else.

An employer is vicariously liable for the negligent acts of his workers under the following circumstances:

- the negligent act must have been carried out by a worker;
- the worker must be an employee;
- the employee must have been acting in the course of his employment, or doing his work, at the time the negligent act was committed.

Example: Rose v Plenty (1976)
Against instructions from his employer, a milkman allowed a 13-year-old boy to assist him with his milk delivery. The boy was injured as a result of the milkman's negligent driving. It was held that the employer was vicariously liable for the milkman's actions as he was acting in the course of his employment when the boy was injured. It was irrelevant that he had disobeyed instructions as he was still doing his job.

> **Crucial tip** An employer will only be vicariously liable for the negligent actions of his employees and not for the negligent actions of his independent contractors.

Quick test
What is vicarious liability?

Section 2   The contract of employment

What are you studying?

This section describes the formation and the contents of a contract of employment. It also identifies the duties of employers and employees with regard to that contract.

How will you be assessed on this?

You will need to know the different types of express and implied terms that are included within the contract of employment.

Crucial concept   A **contract of employment** is like any other contract and it contains both express and implied terms. The contract is made up of terms from a number of different sources.

Express terms

There is no requirement for the contract of employment to be in writing but each employee is required under s. 1 of the *Employment Rights Act 1996* to receive written particulars about his job within two months of the start date. This written statement is referred to as a Section 1 statement. It is not the contract, although the terms contained within it may form part of the contract.

The Section 1 statement must include details of the following:

- names of employer and employee;
- the date employment commenced;
- the date on which continuous employment began;
- the rate and intervals of payment;
- hours of work;
- holiday entitlement and payment;
- sick entitlement and payment;
- pension schemes;
- notice entitlement by both parties;
- title and description of the job;
- how long the job is to last for;
- the place where the employee will be expected to work;
- details of any collective agreement in force.

Other express terms may be stated verbally or included within the contract itself. These terms may include a confidentiality clause so that employees are obliged not to divulge the trade secrets of their employers and a restraint of trade clause to prevent employees from working in competition with their employer either during their employment or after they have left their job.

> **Crucial tip** The date on which employment commenced and the date on which continuous employment began may not be the same. They may be different if, for example, the employee had previously had a number of short-term contracts with the employer.

Implied terms

Terms may be implied into a contract from the following sources:

- common law;
- statute;
- custom and practice.

TERMS IMPLIED UNDER COMMON LAW

Terms may be implied under common law and both employer and employee will have duties imposed upon them. For example, duties imposed upon the employee include the following requirements:

To obey reasonable lawful orders

Example: Pepper v Webb (1969)
A gardener was told by his employer to plant some plants. He refused and swore at the employer. He was held to be in breach of his implied duty to obey a reasonable and lawful order.

The order must be reasonable and lawful, otherwise the employee will not be in breach of contract for refusing to obey it.

Example: Morrish v Henlys Ltd (1973)
An employee was justifed in refusing to obey an unlawful order to falsify accounts.

To act in good faith

Example: Wessex Dairies v Smith (1935)
A milkman was in breach of his duty of good faith when he canvassed his employer's customers on his last day of employment before setting up in business on his own.

To exercise reasonable care and skill

Example: Janata Bank v Ahmed (1981)
A bank manager who approved credit for customers without checking their ability to repay was held to be in breach of his duty of care and skill.

In return, the employer is expected to pay the employee and fulfil the following requirements:

To provide a safe system of work

Example: Pickford v Imperial Chemical Industries PLC (1993)
A secretary suffered repetitive strain injury as a result of working long hours without a break. Her employer was in breach of duty for failing to give advice about the necessity of taking rest breaks.

To provide safe premises and equipment

Example: Bradford v Robinson Rentals (1967)

An employee was required to drive a long distance in bad weather in a vehicle with a broken window and no heater. He suffered frostbite. He was entitled to damages against his employer for breach of duty.

To provide competent fellow staff

Example: Hudson v Ridge Manufacturing Co. Ltd (1957)

An employee was injured as a result of a practical joke played upon him by another employee who was well known for previous similar misconduct. The employer was liable for damages for failure to take sufficient action to curb the misbehaviour of the second employee.

To show mutual trust and confidence in the employee

Example: Isle of Wight Tourist Board v Coombes (1976)

A director's statement to another employee that his secretary was 'an intolerable bitch on a Monday morning' was held to be a breach of trust and confidence.

TERMS IMPLIED BY STATUTE

Terms which are included in some statutes will be implied into the contract of employment regardless of what the contract actually states. For example, terms regarding non-discrimination, minimum periods of notice, minimum rates of pay and health and safety matters are automatically included.

TERMS IMPLIED BY CUSTOM AND PRACTICE

A term may be implied into a contract of employment if it reflects custom and practice in a particular industry.

Quick test

What is a Section 1 statement?

Section 3	Ending the contract of employment

What are you studying?

This section describes the ways in which a contract of employment comes to an end. In particular it describes wrongful dismissal, unfair dismissal and redundancy.

How will you be assessed on this?

You will need to understand how a contract of employment can come to an end and to distinguish between the types of dismissal. You must also understand what happens when the employee believes that the dismissal is wrongful or unfair.

A contract of employment can come to an end in a number of ways. It may be by agreement between the parties, it may be because the employee resigns or it may be because the employee is dismissed. Some dismissals may be lawful but others are not.

Wrongful dismissal

> **Crucial concept**   **Wrongful dismissal** occurs when an employee is dismissed with inadequate notice and there is no apparent contractual reason for the dismissal.

Under s. 86 of the Employment Rights Act 1996, the following minimum periods of notice must be given by the employer:

Duration of employment	Period of notice
Up to 1 month	No notice
1 month – 2 years	1 week
2 years	2 weeks
3 years	3 weeks
4 years – 12 years	1 additional week for each year worked
12 years +	12 weeks

These periods of notice may be increased if specified within the contract of employment. An employee need only give one week's notice unless a higher period is specified within the contract.

If an employee is wrongfully dismissed, he may bring an action against the employer for breach of contract. The usual remedy is damages for the payment he would have received during the notice period.

> **Crucial tip**   Dismissal without notice may be justified under some circumstances, for example if the employee has been dishonest. This type of dismissal is called summary dismissal.

Unfair dismissal

> **Crucial concept**   **Unfair dismissal.** Under s. 94 of the Employment Rights Act 1996, every employee has the right not to be unfairly dismissed.

In order to qualify for this right, the following conditions must apply:

- he must be an employee;

- he must have worked for the employer for a continuous period of one year;

- he must be below 65 or below the normal retirement age;

- he must not be within an excluded category of employment which includes the police and the armed forces;

- he must have brought his claim within three months of the date of dismissal.

> **Crucial tip**   An employee may bring a claim regardless of the number of hours per week that he or she works.

For a dismissal to be fair a two-stage test must be considered:

- Was the reason for dismissal a potentially fair reason?
- Was the reason handled fairly?

WAS THE REASON FOR DISMISSAL A POTENTIALLY FAIR REASON?

The potentially fair reasons are as follows:

Capability

An employee may be deemed incapable if he is incapable of obtaining the necessary qualifications to do the job or because the job performance is incompetent. An employee who is absent on a long-term basis or who is persistently absent for short periods of time may be dismissed for being incapable.

Conduct

A person may be dismissed because of his conduct. Examples of conduct which have been held to justify dismissal include theft, fraud, disobedience of lawful orders and being drunk at work. If the misconduct occurs outside the workplace it should have a direct bearing on the job in order to justify dismissal.

Example: Gardiner v Newport County BC (1974)

A college lecturer who taught students aged 16 to 18 was convicted of gross indecency with another man in a public toilet. His dismissal was held to be fair.

Dismissal may be justified in cases of persistent minor misconduct, for example persistent lateness. However, a series of warnings must have been issued by the employer before the dismissal.

Redundancy

Although redundancy is a potentially fair reason for dismissal, under some circumstances it may be unfair and an employee may have a claim for unfair dismissal. Redundancy is explained in more detail later in this section.

Statutory illegality

A dismissal will be potentially fair if the employee cannot continue with his employment without breaking the law. For example, if a taxi driver is disqualified from driving, his dismissal may be potentially fair.

Some other substantial reason

It is up to the employer to show that the reason for dismissal justified the dismissal of a particular employee. Examples have included cases where there has been a business re-organisation and the employee is not prepared to or is unsuitable to deal with the changes to his contract.

AUTOMATICALLY UNFAIR REASONS FOR DISMISSAL

Some reasons for dismissal are automatically unfair and the employee need not have worked for the employer for the qualifying period of one year in order to bring a claim. These include:

- dismissal for trade union activities;
- dismissal relating to pregnancy and childbirth;

- dismissal relating to health and safety matters;

- dismissal of certain workers who refuse to work on a Sunday;

- dismissal for asserting a statutory right;

- dismissal for making a disclosure about the employer's activities under the Public Interest Disclosure Act 1998.

WAS THE REASON HANDLED FAIRLY?

If the reason for dismissal is potentially fair, the dismissal may still be unfair if:

- the employer did not follow a fair procedure with relation to the reason for dismissal;

- the employer's decision to dismiss did not fall within a range of reasonable responses that would have been made by a reasonable employer.

A fair procedure

The case of *Polkey* v *AE Dayton Services Ltd* (1987), established the principle that a fair procedure must be followed otherwise the employer may not have acted reasonably.

Factors that may be relevant, depending on the reason for dismissal, are:

- If there was more than one offender, were they treated equally?

- Was there was a fair hearing?

- Was alternative employment available?

- Was there an appeal system in operation?

- Was there a system of warnings?

The employment tribunal will consider whether the employer has taken the ACAS Code of Practice (Disciplinary Practice and Procedures in Employment) into account. This gives advice on procedures which employers should take into account where there are minor breaches of contract. The employer should:

- issue a verbal warning;

- issue a first written warning;

- issue a final written warning;

- dismiss.

Range of reasonable responses

The employment tribunal will consider what a reasonable employer under the same circumstances would have done, taking into account the size and the resources available to him. Although some employers may not have dismissed the employee, as long as the decision falls within a range of reasonableness, it will be fair.

Awards for unfair dismissal

If the employment tribunal decides that the employee has been unfairly dismissed, then he may be reinstated to his former job, re-engaged to another job or given compensation.

Compensation is made up of a basic award and a compensatory award. An additional award may also be payable if the tribunal has ordered reinstatement or re-engagement and this has been unreasonably refused by the employer.

The basic award is calculated by multiplying a factor for the employee's age, by the number of years service (to a maximum of 20 years) by the amount of the weekly wage (to a maximum of £240 per week).

The age factor for service is calculated as follows:

- where a person is under 22 = 0.5;

- where a person is 22–41   = 1.0;

- where a person is over 41 = 1.5.

Example
The employee is 48, earns £300 per week and has worked for the employer for 10 years. The calculation would be:

Ages 38 – 41	1.0 x 3 x 240	= £ 720
Ages 41 – 48	1.5 x 7 x 240	= £2,520
	Total =	£3,240

Crucial tip The maximum amount of weekly pay that the employee can claim for is £240, regardless of his actual pay. The age factor will change depending on the age of the employee at the time of service.

The maximum basic award payable is £7,200 (1.5 x 20 x £240).

The compensatory award is an amount that the tribunal believes is just and equitable with regard to the loss sustained by the employee. Such factors as present and future loss of earnings and the age of the applicant will be considered. The maximum amount for the compensatory award is £51,700.

Crucial concept **Redundancy.** This is the dismissal of an employee whose job has ceased to exist.

Redundancy

An employee may be made redundant under one of the following circumstances:

- the business itself ceases to exist;

- the place where the employee works ceases to exist;

- the employee's job ceases to exist;

- fewer employees are required to perform the job.

In order to qualify for a redundancy payment the employee must be under 65 or under the usual retirement age in that business and have two years' continuous service with the employer since the age of 18.

CALCULATING THE REDUNDANCY PAYMENT

The maximum statutory award that may be made is £7,200, although some employers may have their own scheme where payments are in excess of this amount. The payment is calculated in the same way as the basic award for unfair dismissal. The factor for the employee's age is multiplied by the number of years' service (to a maximum of 20 years) and then multiplied by the weekly wage (to a maximum of £240 per week).

REDUNDANCY AND CLAIMS FOR UNFAIR DISMISSAL

An employee who has been made redundant may have a claim for unfair dismissal if redundancy is not the correct reason for the dismissal or if the employer has not followed a proper procedure in selecting for redundancy. For example, there should have been consultation with employees and redeployment should have been considered.

Transfer of undertakings

> Crucial concept   **Transfer of undertakings.** If a business is taken over or the ownership is transferred from one person to another, under the Transfer of Undertakings (Protection of Employment) Regulations 1981, the employees will retain all their statutory employment protection. This is provided that they are in the employment immediately before the transfer took place.

If the employees are dismissed for any reason connected with the transfer they may have a claim for unfair dismissal. The employer may be able to justify the dismissal as fair if he can show an 'economic, technical or organisational' reason for the dismissal, involving a change in the workforce.

Quick test

Explain the difference between wrongful and unfair dismissal.

Section 4	**Discrimination and equal pay**

What are you studying?

This section describes the law relating to discrimination in employment and the law relating to equal pay.

How will you be assessed on this?

You will need to know and be able to describe the main types of discrimination that are unlawful. These are discrimination on the grounds of sex, on the grounds of race and on the grounds of disability. You will also need to know when a person may bring an action under the Equal Pay Act 1970.

Sexual discrimination

> Crucial concept   **Sexual discrimination.** Under the Sex Discrimination Act 1975, as amended by the Sex Discrimination Act 1986, it is unlawful to discriminate on the grounds of a person's sex or because a person is married. The Act applies equally to men and women, but a man cannot bring an action where special treatment is afforded to women in connection with pregnancy or childbirth. The Act applies both to applicants for jobs and to employees.

There are three types of discrimination:

- direct discrimination;
- indirect discrimination;
- victimisation.

DIRECT DISCRIMINATION

This is where a person is treated less favourably than someone of the opposite sex or is treated less favourably than someone who is married.

Example: Batisha v Say (1977)
A woman who applied for a job as a cave guide was turned down on the grounds that the work was not suitable for a woman. It was held by the tribunal that there had been direct discrimination against her.

Sexual harassment is not defined within the 1975 Act, but any unwanted sexual attention by one person towards another may amount to direct discrimination. It must be shown that a person of the opposite sex would not have been subjected to the same treatment.

Example: Porcelli v Strathclyde Regional Council (1986)
A woman who worked as a laboratory technician was subjected to personal insults and sexual harassment by two male colleagues who wanted to force her to leave her job. It was held that she had been a victim of direct discrimination.

INDIRECT DISCRIMINATION

This occurs where an employer applies a requirement or condition which would apply equally to a man or woman, but:

● the proportion of one sex which may comply with it is considerably smaller than the proportion within the other sex;

● it cannot be shown to be justified irrespective of the sex of the person to whom it is applied; and

● it is to the person's detriment that they cannot comply with it.

Example: Price v Civil Service Commission (1978)
The Civil Service advertised for staff aged between $17^1/_2$ and 28. The age limits applied equally to men and women. However, Mrs Price argued that fewer women than men could comply with such a requirement because they would have been bringing up children.

VICTIMISATION

This occurs where a person is treated less favourably because he or she has brought an action or has been involved in an action under the Sex Discrimination Act 1975.

EXCEPTIONS TO THE SEX DISCRIMINATION ACT 1975

In certain cases an employer is permitted to treat members of one sex more favourably than members of the other sex. The main exceptions are contained within s. 7 and are referred to as s. 7 'genuine occupational qualifications'. These apply as follows:

● when the job requires male or female characteristics, e.g. modelling.

● when there are issues of decency or privacy;

● where there is close personal contact;

● where the employee lives in and it is unreasonable to expect additional facilities to be provided;

● in single sex establishments where the inmates require special care or supervision;

● where the job involves personal services relating to education or welfare;

- where the job requires working in another country where custom or law forbids work by one sex;

- where the job is one of two held by a married couple.

Racial discrimination

> **Crucial concept**   **Racial discrimination.** Under the Race Relations Act 1976 it is unlawful to discriminate against someone on the grounds of their race. Racial grounds are defined in s. 3 as colour, race, nationality or ethnic or national origins. The Act applies to both job applicants and employees.

There are three types of discrimination which mirror those defined within the Sex Discrimination Act 1975.

DIRECT DISCRIMINATION
This occurs where a person is treated less favourably on the grounds of his or her race.

INDIRECT DISCRIMINATION
This occurs where a requirement or condition applies equally to all races, but:

- the proportion of one race that may comply with it is considerably smaller than those from other races; *and*

- it cannot be shown to be justified; *and*

- it is to the person's detriment that he or she cannot comply with it.

VICTIMISATION
This occurs where a person is treated less favourably because he or she has brought an action or has been involved in an action under the Race Relations Act 1976.

EXCEPTIONS TO THE RACE RELATIONS ACT 1976
The main exceptions, which again are referred to as 'genuine occupational qualifications', are contained within s. 5(2). These are:

- where the job involves acting or entertainment;

- jobs as artists and photographers' models;

- where the job involves serving food and a particular race is required to give authenticity;

- where personal and welfare services are provided for certain racial groups.

Bringing an action under the Sex Discrimination Act 1975 and the Race Relations Act 1976
A complaint must be made to the employment tribunal within three months of the incident, although this period may be extended if the tribunal thinks it just and equitable to do so. The tribunal may:

- declare the person's rights have been infringed;

- order compensation (the amount of the award is unlimited and compensation can cover injury to feelings);

- recommend that the employer remove the discrimination.

Disability discrimination

> Crucial concept — The **Disability Discrimination Act** 1995 outlaws discrimination against disabled people. A person is disabled under s. 1 of the Act if he: '. . . has a physical or mental impairment which has a substantial and long-term adverse affect on his ability to carry out normal day-to-day activities.'

The 1995 Act applies to those who have a contract with an employer, so it covers both employees and independent contractors. The Act does not apply where less than 15 people are employed. Only direct discrimination and victimisation are covered by the Act.

DIRECT DISCRIMINATION

This occurs when an employer treats a disabled person less favourably than he would treat another without such a disability and he cannot justify that discrimination.

The employer has a duty to make reasonable adjustments to deal with the needs of the disabled worker. This may include altering premises and equipment and changing a disabled worker's working hours. It must be reasonable for the employer to take such steps and certain matters will be taken into account such as the extent of the employer's resources and how practical it is for him to take these steps.

VICTIMISATION

This occurs when a person is treated less favourably because he or she has brought an action or has been involved in an action under the Disability Discrimination Act 1995.

Bringing an action under the Disability Discrimination Act 1995

A complaint must be made to the employment tribunal within three months of the incident. The tribunal may:

- make a declaration as to the rights of the complainant or the employer;
- order compensation (again the amount of the award is unlimited and can include injury to feelings);
- recommend that the employer takes action within a particular period of time.

Vicarious liability and discrimination

Employers may be vicariously liable for actions by employees carried out in the course of their employment which are in contravention of the Sex Discrimination Act 1975, the Race Relations Act 1976 or the Disability Discrimination Act 1995.

Equal pay

> Crucial concept — Under the **Equal Pay Act** 1970, men and women should receive the same pay for doing the same work. The 1970 Act was amended by the Equal Pay (Amendment) Regulations 1983 to comply with an Equal Pay Directive under EU law. In theory a person can now bring an action under the Equal Pay Act 1970 or under Article 141 of the Treaty of Rome.

In order to bring an action a woman must be able to compare herself with a man in the same type of work. She must show one of the following:

- that she is employed on *like work* to his;

- that she is employed on *work rated as equivalent* to his;

- if neither of the above apply, her work must be of *equal value* to his.

> Crucial tip   Although the 1970 Act refers to women comparing themselves to men, it applies equally to men and women.

LIKE WORK

This means that the work must be broadly similar and the differences should not be of any practical importance.

Example: Shields v *Coombes (Holdings) Ltd* (1978)
Men who worked in a betting shop were paid more than women who worked there as they were said to be responsible for preventing trouble. As there had never been any trouble the difference in their jobs was of no practical importance.

WORK RATED AS EQUIVALENT

Work will be rated as equivalent if it has been given the same rating under a job evaluation scheme.

EQUAL VALUE

If the work is not like work or work rated as equivalent, the woman may claim she is doing work of equal value. The tribunal must consider the demands made upon the woman and on the man she is compared with. The case may be referred to an independent expert for his opinion.

Example: Hayward v *Cammell Laird Shipbuilders* (1988)
A female cook claimed that her work was of equal value to men working as painters, joiners and thermal engineers. Although her basic wage was lower, she received better sickness benefit, paid meal breaks and better holiday entitlement. However, the House of Lords held that each term of the contract must be considered separately and her claim was successful.

THE GENUINE MATERIAL FACTOR DEFENCE

An employer may have a defence to a claim for equal pay if he can show that there is a genuine material factor, not based upon sex, which was responsible for the difference. Examples may include length of service and academic qualifications.

Quick test

What are the main statutes which cover the law relating to discrimination in employment?

Crucial examples

1. (a) What is the difference between an employee and an independent contractor?
   (b) Bill, who is employed by ZX Deliverers, is driving from A to B to deliver goods. On route he diverts to C to visit his mother. As he leaves C he fails to notice a stationary car, and drives into the back of it. Bob, the owner of the car wishes to sue ZX Deliverers. Under what circumstances will they be responsible for Bill's actions?

2. How may terms be implied into a contract of employment?

3. (a) How may a contract of employment come to an end?

(b) When may an employee have a claim for unfair dismissal?

(c) When may an employee have a claim for wrongful dismissal?

(d) When may an employee be made redundant?

4. (a) When is an employer permitted to treat members of one sex more favourably than members of another?

(b) What types of discrimination are contrary to the Sex Discrimination Act 1975 and the Race Relations Act 1976?

(c) Who may bring an action under the Race Relations Act 1976?

(d) What evidence must a woman produce if she wants to make a successful claim under the Equal Pay Act 1970?

Answers

1. (a) An employee is employed by an employer and works under a contract of service. An independent contractor is self-employed and works under a contract for service.

(b) For an employer to be vicariously liable for the negligent acts of his employee, three things must be shown;

- the negligent act must have been carried out by the worker;
- the worker must be an employee;
- the employee must have been acting in the course of his employment.

Applied here, Bill, an employee, appears to have been negligent by driving into a stationary car. It is unlikely that he was acting in the course of his employment as he has diverted to C to visit his mother. A claim against ZX Deliverers would probably fail.

2. Terms may be implied into the contract by common law, statute and custom and practice.

3. (a) A contract of employment may come to an end by agreement between the parties, by resignation or by dismissal.

(b) An employee may have a claim for unfair dismissal if he has worked for his employer for a continuous period of one year and he is below 65 or the normal retirement age. The reason for dismissal must not be one of the potentially fair reasons and the claim must be brought within three months of the date of dismissal.

(c) An employee may have a claim for wrongful dismissal if he is dismissed without notice and there is no reason for the dismissal.

(d) An employee can be made redundant if the business ceases to exist, the place where the employee works ceases to exist, the employee's job ceases to exist or fewer employees are required to perform the job.

4. (a) An employer is permitted to treat members of one sex more favourably when one of the exceptions contained within s. 7 of the Sex Discrimination Act 1975 apply. These are known as genuine occupational qualifications.

(b) The types of discrimination are direct discrimination, indirect discrimination and victimisation.

(c) A job applicant or an employee who is discriminated against on the grounds of his race may bring an action under the 1976 Act.

(d) For a succesful claim under the 1970 Act a woman must be able to compare herself with a man in the same type of work. She must show that she is employed on like work or work rated as equivalent or that her work is of equal value.

Crucial reading and research

Holland and Burnett, *Legal Practice Course Guide to Employment Law*, 8th edn., Oxford University Press.

Smith and Thomas, *Smith & Wood's Industrial Law*, 7th edn., Butterworths.

AND ANSWERS

This chapter is designed to test your ability to answer questions in a variety of forms. It allows you to practice answering multiple choice questions (MCQ's), problem questions and essay-type questions. It requires you to demonstrate your knowledge across a variety of subjects covered in this book.

Examination technique
It is not enough when answering examination questions merely to identify the legal issues involved and write all you know about that topic. A good answer should show a knowledge of legal rules and principles and be able to apply them to the question. You need to be able to distinguish between the irrelevant and the relevant legal points. You need to be able to construct an argument to answer a question. It is no good simply writing down all the points that you think are important if it isn't coherent and logical. For example, in a problem question if you are asked to advise one party or consider the rights and liabilities of several parties, it is no good simply writing down all the law you know on the subject and then adding a final sentence saying here is the law sort it out for yourselves. If you are asked to advise parties you need to offer them the pros and cons of the legal solutions that might be available to them.

Students often find developing the technique for answering problem questions difficult. This is where your attendance at seminars is important because this will be a place where you will have the opportunity to develop a technique. Students avoid problem questions in the belief that they are difficult but if you have the legal knowledge and develop the technique for answering them, high marks can be gained as you can demonstrate legal knowledge and method.

Students commonly believe that essay-type questions are easier because they can simply write all they know about a given topic. This approach will not produce good answers and earn you good marks. To begin with, essay questions usually require a thorough knowledge of a topic and an ability to construct a well-structured answer. When was the last time you saw an essay question that said 'write all you know about consideration in contract'? Beware, essay questions often require you to express views and opinions or make critical observations upon a subject and if you are not familiar and confident with that subject you will not produce a good answer. Being able to test and marshal your thoughts and opinions on a given legal subject in seminars is a good way to prepare yourself for answering essay questions.

With the advent of MCQ's it is no longer possible for students to simply pick specific topics and concentrate their revision on these areas. MCQ's demand a broad general knowledge of all the topics dealt with in your studies. Students who have to sit examinations with MCQ's on the paper must develop a broad based approach to their studies. Often that breadth of knowledge helps when it comes to essay and problem questions as a good student may be able to draw upon his or her general legal knowledge when addressing particular topics. For example, in answering an exclusion clause question in contract the good student may be able to draw upon knowledge of supply of goods and services to enhance the answer.

Do not forget that this text is only setting out the basics of the legal knowledge you should be acquiring in your studies. The detailed legal knowledge, case law and the skills you need to produce really good answers in examinations will come from your lectures, seminars and be developed with your tutor's help.

Section I	Mutiple choice questions

Choose one answer from the four possible solutions.

1. A creditor can petition for a debtor's bankruptcy if the debtor owes more than:
   (a) £300
   (b) £500
   (c) £750
   (d) £1,500

2. What is the standard of proof that must be established to secure a criminal conviction against an accused?
   (a) On the balance of probabilities the accused must be guilty.
   (b) It must be proved to the satisfaction of the trial judge that the accused is guilty.
   (c) It must be proved beyond reasonable doubt that the accused is guilty.
   (d) It must be established that the accused is guilty to the standard that the reasonable person would accept.

3. In the following, indicate which situation might result in civil proceedings:
   (a) Diane returns a faulty steam iron to the shop where she bought it and the manager refuses to give her a refund.
   (b) Colin is given a parking ticket by a traffic warden for parking on a double yellow line.
   (c) Jane drives through a 30mph area at 50mph and is detected by speed cameras, resulting in a summons for speeding.
   (d) None of the above.

4. A voidable contract is:
   (a) unenforceble

(b) illegal
(c) regarded as a nullity
(d) valid unless and until one of the parties takes steps to avoid it.

5. A partnership must have a partnership deed:
(a) if there are more than 20 partners
(b) if there are less than 20 partners
(c) if the partners want a partnership deed
(d) if the partnership is to continue for more than one year.

6. Company members can remove a company director by passing:
(a) a special resolution
(b) a written resolution
(c) an extraordinary resolution
(d) an ordinary resolution.

7. Arthur, Adam and Alan run an electrical repair business known as 'Triple A Electrics Ltd'. Is it:
(a) A private limited company?
(b) A partnership?
(c) A public limited company?
(d) A sole trader enterprise?

8. Robin hires a garden rotivator for the weekend. It breaks down at 5.30pm on Saturday evening due to a faulty motor part. Robin cannot get it replaced because the hire shop is closed and does not reopen till 9.30 on Monday morning (when Robin will be back at work). Robin considers he is entitled to some compensation for not being able to use the rotivator over the weekend. Should he complain about the rotivator's unsatisfactory performance under:
(a) The Supply of Goods and Services Act 1982?
(b) The Consumer Protection Act 1987?
(c) The Unfair Contract Terms Act 1977?
(d) The Sale of Goods Act 1979?

9. Usually cases concerning employment law are dealt with:
(a) by the magistrates' court
(b) by the county court
(c) by arbitration
(d) by tribunal.

10. In the tort of negligence if a defendant claims the claimant was *volenti non fit injuria* does this mean:
(a) The claimant agreed not to sue the defendant in the event of injury?
(b) The claimant knew there was a risk of injury and consented to run that risk?
(c) The claimant knew there was a risk of injury?
(d) The defendant was not negligent?

11. In the case of *Donoghue* v *Stevenson* the claimant was able to pursue a claim in negligence against the maker of the contaminated ginger beer which she consumed because:
(a) she had a contract with the manufacturer
(b) she had a contract with the café owner
(c) the manufacturer is liable for every injury that results from his carelessness
(d) the manufacturer should have foreseen that the claimant would be affected by his actions.

12. Sue, who works for 'Flowers to your Door Ltd', was delivering a bouquet to Annie's house

when she negligently backed the company's van out of Annie's drive and hit Annie's neighbour's car which was parked on the road outside. Who is liable for the damage to the neighbour's car?

(a) Sue because she should have backed out with more care.

(b) 'Flowers to your Door' because Sue caused the damage whilst she was working.

(c) Annie because it was her drive Sue was backing out of.

(d) The neighbour because she shouldn't have parked on the road next to Annie's drive.

Section 2 — Essay and problem questions

1. Describe the main sources of English law today.

2. Describe three of the main institutions of the European Community and comment upon the roles they play in the working of the EU.

3. Alan restores and sells antique agricultural and garden machinery. On Tuesday Bella brings in a very old lawnmower which she suggests could be worth £150 and asks him if he would be interested in buying it. Upon examining it Alan thinks it might be a very rare model which could be worth as much as £700. He doesn't tell Bella its true worth in case she asks for more than £150 so he says to her he will think about it for a day or so and then let her know if he wants it.

   On Wednesday morning Alan writes to Bella offering to buy the lawnmower for £150. By the time his letter arrives on Thursday Bella has spoken to an old market gardener whose hobby is restoring old garden machinery. He tells her it worth a lot more than £150. Bella therefore ignores Alan's letter and decides to put the lawnmower in a local auction to see what it will fetch. Alan discovers what she has done and rings her up saying that as he has agreed to pay her asking price of £150 he considers she is bound to sell it to him at that price.

   Advise Bella as to whether she must sell to Alan. Explain the reasons for your advice.

4. Angela buys a 'Plum' personal computer from Byte Ltd. She signs a sales note in the shop saying 'Any express or implied condition, statement or warranty, statutory or otherwise is hereby excluded'. She uses the PC for a week satisfactorily but then it no longer works properly.

   What are Angela's legal rights if:

   (a) she bought the computer for personal use;

   (b) Angela is an accountant and bought the computer so that she could work from home?

5. A bathing costume priced £49 was advertised for sale in a shop as 'super new lycra fit swimsuit keeps its shape swim after swim'. Helen bought it, wore it once and found that after washing it once, according to the manufacturer's instructions, it lost its shape and stretched. She has been unable to wear it again.

   Helen wants to know if she can get her money back. Advise Helen as to her legal rights.

6. Elaine employed Barry to redecorate her bedroom. When Barry was part way through the job, Elaine noticed that some of the wallpaper was a slightly different shade of green to the rest. When she asked Barry about this he said he had bought it from a decorators' merchant and it was all from the same batch as far as he knew.

   Elaine said she wasn't happy about the colour variation and wanted it all matching. Barry said it wasn't his fault the wallpaper was not all perfectly matched and she would have to take the matter up with the decorators' merchant or the wallpaper manufacturers.

   Advise Elaine.

7. Plantline Ltd are employed by the newly refurbished Wellfields Health Centre to landscape the front gardens of the building. There is a lot of equipment on site and the workmen are told at the end of each day equipment and materials are to be locked up in the site compound. However, because it is a health centre, the workmen are told that a safe access has to be maintained to the health centre at all times, during its opening hours.

One afternoon it is raining very heavily and the access path to the health centre becomes very slippery and wet with mud from the workmen's feet and equipment. Harold, an elderly, arthritic patient who is visiting the health centre for an appointment, slips on the pathway and breaks his leg upon falling. As a result of this fall he ends up spending six weeks in hospital and suffers considerable pain as a result of the injury.

One evening after work, the workmen do not clear up a pile of broken slabs which they intend to get rid of the following morning. They also leave a garden roller outside the locked compound.

Jenny and Chris, aged nine and ten, are playing in the area after the health centre has closed. They go on site. Jenny climbs on the broken slabs and they fall, landing on the garden roller, which rolls forward and traps Chris' foot. In her panic to get help for Chris, Jenny falls off the pile of broken slabs and sprains her ankle. The children have to call to a passer-by for help. She comes on site and has to push the garden roller off Chris' foot to free him. As a result of this action she hurts her back and has to spend the following week off work to recover.

Advise Harold, Chris and Jenny, and the passer by as to any claims they may have in respect of their injuries.

Who would they make their claims against and upon what grounds?

8. (a) You are consulted by a client who is the sole proprietor of a successful confectionery business. The main assets of the business are the land on which the factory stands together with the plant and machinery involved in the production of sweets.

Your client indicates that his daughter wishes to take an active part in the management of the business. He is agreeable to this and is prepared to allow his daughter an interest in the business but he wants to retain control of it.

Your client's daughter has recently inherited a large amount of money from a distant relative. He wants to ensure that her financial situation will be safeguarded if the confectionery trade suffers in a recession.

Advise your client as to the type of business association which would be most appropriate for him and his daughter. Describe the legal implications of each option available to him and which would be most appropriate for his needs.

(b) Another client advises you that his brother-in-law, who has recently taken early retirement from a corporate managerial post, wants to invest £30,000 in a business venture and has approached him about putting money into his paper recycling business. His brother-in-law has also suggested that he would like to become involved in the business on a part-time basis.

Your client would not object to further investment in his business but does not want his brother-in-law to have any real say in the running of the business. His brother-in-law's chief objective is to obtain a regular source of income from his investment.

Can you find a compromise solution to this situation which suits both your client and his brother-in-law?

9. Jack and Gill want to set up a company to make and sell garden gnomes.
   (a) What kind of company would be suitable for their purposes?
   (b) Would they need any other members before they could establish a company?
   (c) Could Jack be managing director and company secretary?
   (d) If they were both directors would they have to employ someone to be company secretary?

(e) Could they advertise the company shares for sale in a local newspaper?

10. What is the difference between a contract of service and a contract for services? Why is it important to distinguish between the two for employment law purposes?

Answers

Mutiple choice questions

1. c.
2. c.
3. a.
4. d.
5. c.
6. d
7. a.
8. a.
9. d
10. b
11. d.
12. b

Essay and problem questions

1. See Chapter 1, Sections 3 and 4.

This is an essay type question which asks you to 'describe' the sources. You need to name the sources: common law, statute/legislation, European Union law and describe the part each plays in the English legal system.

Common law is sometimes known as case law or judge-made law so you need to know the alternative ways it may be referred to. You should explain how the doctrine of judicial precedent is important in the common law.

When discussing statutes you could identify it as law enacted by the Queen in Parliament. You do not need to go into detail as to how a Bill becomes an Act of Parliament. You should write about parliamentary sovereignty and explain what this means. A good student would be able to explain how Parliament can make whatever laws it pleases and the courts cannot change statutes but are bound to apply the law enacted by Parliament. This would show that the student understood the importance of statutes as a source of law.

When describing EU law as a source it would be useful to place EU law in context by explaining the legal obligations the UK took on when it joined the European Community. Where EU law conflicts with UK legislation, EU law takes precedence. This shows that the supremacy of the UK Parliament is not absolute. The sources of Community law should be named: (Treaties, Regulations, Directives and Decisions) and the student should describe how each takes effect. A good student may gain more marks by giving examples of these sources. For example the Treaty of Maastricht or the directive on Unfair Terms in Consumer Contracts.

A good student would also recognise the importance of the Human Rights Act 1998 and the impact it has upon existing legislation. UK legislation must now be interpreted as far as possible by the courts in a way which is compatible with the Convention Rights.

2. See Chapter 1, Section 3.

This is an essay-type question which asks you to describe three EC institutions and comment on their roles.

You could choose three from the following:

- The Council of Ministers;

- The Commission;
- European Parliament;
- European Court of Justice.

A common problem that occurs when students attempt to answer this type of question is that they can name the institutions but don't really know what they do or what role they play in the working of the EC.

A good student should be able to explain what each institution does and give examples of the work the various institutions undertake. For example the Council of Ministers is made up of appropriate Ministers from each Member State depending upon what subject is under discussion. For instance, following the BSE and foot and mouth crises in agriculture the Agricultural Ministers of the various states met to discuss these issues. If there are major policy decisions, such as admitting new Member States to the EU, the heads of government from each State will attend a Council meeting to discuss such issues.

As the question asks what part each institution plays in the working of the EU it is important to be able to explain their relative importance. For example, it would be useful to demonstrate that you know that the Council of Ministers is very important because it considers legislative proposals put forward by the Commission, whereas the European Parliament, which has members elected from each State does not have legislative powers and therefore has far less influence. A good student should be able to make comparison with the UK Parliament which does have legislative powers.

3. See Chapter 2, Section 1.

This is a problem question which asks you to advise Bella and explain why you have given her this advice. First, you need to identify the area of law you should be dealing with. In this case it is offer and acceptance. Do not simply write out the rules you can remember for offer and acceptance. Apply your knowledge to the question and only use the relevant parts.

Answering a question like this is rather like answering a mathematics question. The examiner is interested in whether you get to the right answer but is just as interested in how you got there. If you simply say there is no contract therefore Bella doesn't have to sell the lawnmower to Alan you won't get very good marks but if you can show your reasons as to why you came to this conclusion the examiner will be much more impressed.

For example, you may start by saying there was an invitation to treat when Bella asked Alan if he was interested in buying the lawnmower. The offer doesn't come until Wednesday when Alan makes a written offer to Bella. Alan's offer must be accepted by Bella and Alan cannot assume that he has a contract merely because he offered to buy the lawnmower for the price Bella was seeking initially. As Bella does not communicate any acceptance to Alan, there is no contract. Therefore Bella does not have to sell the lawnmower to Alan.

A good student would support these points with appropriate cases.

4. See Chapter 2, Section 2 and Chapter 3, Section 2.

This is a problem question which asks you to consider Angela's legal rights. You would need to identify that this question features the use of an exclusion clause in the contract. However, the good student would also be aware that the question requires a demonstration of some knowledge of the Sale of Goods Act 1979 implied terms too. Students who simply pick a limited number of topics to revise for examination purposes would find themselves disadvantaged in answering a question like this if they hadn't covered contract and sale of goods issues.

As with question 3, you need to try to find a solution to the problem and demonstrate how you came to that conclusion. Identify what an exclusion clause does when it is introduced into a contract. You should check whether the clause would be valid at common law. For instance, did Angela know of the clause before signing the contract. In this case she appears to be aware of it as it is written on a sales note which she signed. The question asks about two senarios. This should alert you to the fact that the application of the exclusion clause rules may differ depending upon whether she bought the computer as a consumer or in a business capacity.

It would be necessary to consider what rights Angela may have when her computer breaks down. Reference should be made to s. 14 of the Sale of Goods Act 1979. A good student should be able to explain what s. 14 says, that goods bought from a business seller should be of satisfactory quality and fit for their purpose. If Angela's computer does not work properly after one week, it would not appear to be of satisfactory quality nor fit for its purpose.

Under normal circumstances a breach of s. 14(2) and (3) would entitle Angela to return the goods and get her money back but you would have to ask whether she has lost her right to complain about the goods because of the exclusion clause she signed, which stated that 'implied condition . . . hereby excluded'. Although this may have taken her rights away at common law she can use the Unfair Contract Terms Act 1977 which is a statutory means of controlling exclusion clauses.

At this point you would need to deal with the two different senarios:

(a) As a consumer (defined under s. 12 of the 1977 Act) Angela is covered by s. 6 (2) of the Act which provides that ss. 13–15 of the Sale of Goods Act 1979 cannot be excluded or restricted in a consumer sale by any contract term. Therefore Angela can take her computer back and ask for a refund.

(b) Where Angela is working as an accountant from home this would mean she is not a consumer within the meaning of s. 12 of the 1977 Act. Although a business seller can include a contract term which would exclude or limit her rights contained in ss. 13–15 of the Sale of Goods Act 1979 this can only be done if the term is reasonable. What is reasonable is defined in s. 11 and sch. 2 of the 1977 Act. On balance this exclusion clause is so wide that it would not be regarded as reasonable and so Angela would still be able to return her computer and ask for a refund.

This question is a good example of a problem-type question that requires you to demonstrate a good depth of knowledge in two topic areas. It is a question, which if answered well could attract very high marks but students who attempt to answer it without reference to the appropriate Acts and sections will not do well. Too often students try to answer questions of this sort without any real knowledge of the appropriate statutes.

5. See Chapter 3, Section 2.

This is a problem question which requires you to advise Helen as to her legal rights. You will need to identify that this is a Sale of Goods Act 1979 question requiring knowledge of the implied terms.

It looks as if Helen is a consumer so you could consider what her rights would be if there was a breach of the implied terms. The implied terms are conditions of the contract. A breach of an implied term means she could return the goods and ask for her money back.

Identify which implied terms you think may have been broken.

Section 13 – goods must correspond with their description when the buyer relies on the description. There is nothing to suggest Helen did not rely on the description. Therefore she would expect the swimsuit to keep its shape after washing. A questioning student may raise the point that the description states the swimsuit keeps its shape after swimming, not after washing, so the seller might argue that there is no breach, although it would be difficult to sustain such an argument.

Helen could also claim, under s. 14(2) of the Act, that the swimsuit is not of satisfactory quality. She clearly purchased the item in a shop which means it was sold in the course of a business. The good student should then be able to state what kind of things would be expected of goods that are of satisfactory quality. In this case she would be looking particularly at appearance and fitness for purpose. If the swimsuit has lost its shape and has become unwearable then it would appear to fail the satisfactory quality standard that a reasonable person would expect of such a garment. A good candidate should be able to refer to a case such as *Rogers v Parish* (1987) as an example.

Helen may also say there is a breach of s. 14(3) and the swimsuit is not fit for its purpose. The purpose is fairly obvious. She should expect to be able to swim in the swimsuit and presumably wash it afterwards.

You should conclude that Helen probably has a good case for saying that there has been a breach of s. 13 and s. 14. She should expect to get her money back if she returns the goods.

This is not the type of question that you should attempt unless you can identify the area of law involved. You should be able to refer to the Sale of Goods Act 1979 and the relevant sections. It is not enough to simply say that the goods are unfit and not of satisfactory quality. You must know why. What can a consumer expect?

Sometimes students with a poor knowledge of the implied terms will not recognise that the consumer's remedy lies with the seller. It is not relevant to discuss the manufacturer's liability in negligence.

6. See Chapter 3, Section 6.

This is a problem question which requires you to advise Elaine. You will need to know that this is about the supply of goods and services and reference should be made to the Supply of Goods and Services Act 1982. Elaine is paying for Barry's services as a decorator and he will supply the wallpaper (the materials) with the service. Although the remedies for breach of implied terms covering the materials supplied are almost the same as those under the Sale of Goods Act 1979, the good student will know that it is s. 4 of the Supply of Goods and Services Act 1982 when materials are not of satisfactory quality. You should identify why the wallpaper is unsatisfactory – its appearance appears to be the issue as it is mismatched.

The good student should be able to explain why Elaine has a remedy against Barry and does not have to take the matter up with the manufacturer as Barry suggests. It is Barry's responsibility to supply materials of satisfactory quality just as it would be with any business seller.

A student with a good knowledge of the 1982 Act may go on to question whether Barry is carrying out his trade with the care and skill you would expect of a competent decorator. (see s. 13 of the Supply of Goods and Services Act 1982). Perhaps he should have realised that the paper was mismatched and taken steps himself to sort it out. Students with a poor knowledge of the Act and the appropriate sections will not be able to answer the question well. Some students with poor knowledge of this area may confuse the Sale of Goods Act 1979 and the Supply of Goods and Services Act 1982.

7. See Chapter 4, Sections 1–3 and Chapter 7, Section 1.

This is a problem question which requires you to advise various claimants in respect of injuries they sustain. You need to identify that this is a question about the tort of negligence. You cannot tackle a problem question of this sort without having an understanding of what a tort is and what a claimant needs to prove to establish a negligence claim.

Students often refer to the case of *Donoghue v Stevenson* and talk about the defendant owing the claimant a duty of care but do not go on to ask if that duty has been broken and whether resultant damage has occurred. You cannot simply say X owes Y a duty of care and therefore Y can make a claim against X. It is important in a negligence claim to consider what the defendant may be liable for. You cannot assume that all the damage suffered by a claimant is the defendant's fault. There must be a link between the damage caused and the breach of duty (look at the 'but for' test).

In this question a good student would recognise that vicarious liability is also an issue and that the claimants would make their claims against Plantline Ltd, the employers, and not the employees.

To establish whether a duty of care was owed to the claimants a good student would refer to the case of *Donoghue* v *Stevenson* and in particular to Lord Atkin's 'neighbour principle'. A less perceptive student would probably refer to the case but simply recite the facts. This would not really add anything useful to the answer.

Based on the neighbour principle Harold would be owed a duty of care. The workmen should have kept the access to the health centre clear and safe for use. Using the tests laid down to establish whether there was a breach of duty it should be possible to argue that it should have been reasonably foreseeable that patients, some of whom would be old and frail, would need access to the health centre and would be vulnerable to the risk of injury if the access wasn't kept clear. The workmen's breach of duty, by failing to keep the access clear, could lead to accidents. Harold's injuries were a direct result of their breach and therefore Harold is likely to make a successful claim against Plantline Ltd.

As regards Jenny and Chris, a less thoughtful student may dismiss a claim by them on the basis that they should not have been playing on site when the health centre was closed. However, based on the neighbour principle, a duty of care exists towards those who you should consider may be affected by your actions. Children are particularly vulnerable and the defendants in this case should have considered the likelihood of children being attracted to an open building site. Presumably Plantline Ltd specified that all equipment should be locked up at the end of the day so that this type of incident would not happen. Therefore it would appear that Plantline Ltd thought it might be reasonably foreseeable that some people could be at risk even after the health centre had closed if they didn't lock away all their equipment. Looking at the tests for breach of duty it would appear that adequate precautions were not taken and therefore a breach of duty did occur which resulted in the children being injured. Jenny and Chris are likely to make a successful claim.

Finally, there is the question of liability towards the passer-by who came to the children's aid. Initially you might feel that she didn't need to be on site and she put herself at risk and her injuries were caused by her own actions not as a consequence of anything Plantline did or didn't do. However, if you argue that she came on site to rescue the children who were physically at risk, Plantline could owe her a duty of care which was breached, and her injuries were as a direct result of their negligence. Applying the 'but for' test you could argue that but for the actions of the defendants the claimant would not have been injured because she would not have had to come to the aid of the children. In other words, she would not have been in that position had it not been for the actions of the Plantline workmen.

Although this seems a detailed and complex question involving many aspects of negligence, once you have grasped the basic foundations of duty, breach and damage all you have to do is apply them in each instance.

8. See Chapter 5, Sections 1–3.

This is a problem question in two parts asking you to advise the clients. It requires you to have a good general knowledge of the differences between various business organisations and an ability to compare and contrast the advantages and disadvantages of operating in the different business organisations.

Part (a) requires that you assess your client's requirements in relation to working as a sole trader, in partnership or as a limited liability company.

A basic answer would simply go through the advantages and disadvantages of each type of business organisation. A better answer would look at the client's requests and see which organisation best fitted his needs pointing out the pros and cons of each type of organisation.

The client does not want his daughter's finances put at risk therefore he would not want to enter into a partnership based upon the 1890 Partnership Act. This would mean his daughter would have unlimited liability. He would also lose overall control of his business if he had to accept her as an equal partner. A good student may be able to discuss the Limited Liability Partnership Act 2000 and the Limited Partnership Act 1907 as options, as they would give his daughter some financial protection. Some students may dismiss his remaining as a sole trader because they might argue that this gives his daughter no interest in the business. A student who has considered all the options carefully may argue that this option may be made to work for them as his daughter would not have any requirement to invest and yet could be offered a job as an employee with management responsibilities. This option may prove attractive to the client as it would be the least disruptive option. The client could still control the business and his daughter's personal finances would not be put at risk at all.

A viable option may be the setting up of a limited liability company where the daughter could buy shares and therefore have an interest in the business without risking anything but her share capital. She could be offered preference shares which would limit her right to vote otherwise her father would have to make sure he retained over 75% of the shares so that she could not prevent him passing special resolutions. If she wanted to take part in the running of the company he could offer her a directorship and/or the company secretary's job. He would probably want to be appointed managing director in order to maintain control of the company. However, if he converts his business to a limited liability company it will cost him some financial outlay and he will have to comply with company law requirements as to appropriate documentation and annual return requirements. The client may not think the benefits of being a limited liability company are sufficient to justify the expense, reorganisation and legal requirements.

Part (b) asks you to consider various business options but with slightly different considerations. In this case a good student would be aware that if the brother-in-law invested capital in the business and took part in managing it, he and the client may have created a partnership whether they intended to or not. If there was a partnership the brother-in-law would be an agent of the firm. This would deprive the client of his overall control of the business. As for the brother-in-law receiving a regular income, there could be no guarantee of this as partners are paid out of profits and if there are no profits, there is no income. Also the brother-in-law's finances would be at risk as he would have unlimited liability.

Another option would be to convert the business into a limited liability company. The client could offer his brother-in-law shares but they would have to be preference shares if the brother-in-law wanted a regular income from them and the client didn't want him to have any voting rights in the company. (You would have to have a reasonably good knowledge of company law to pick up on this point.) It would be possible to employ his brother-in-law on a part-time basis in the company. This would all be subject to the client being willing to covert his business to a limited liability company.

Finally, you could consider the client remaining as a sole trader, employing his brother-in-law in some capacity and taking a secured loan from his brother-in-law if he wanted further investment for his business. A secured loan could give his brother-in-law a regular return on his money in the form of interest and allow the client to retain control of his business, without having to change his business operation.

9. See Chapter 6, Sections 1 and 2.
   This is a relatively easy question. It isn't quite an essay question but it certainly is not a complex problem question. It simply requires you to demonstrate an awareness of different types of companies and their particular characteristics and apply that to the

question. However, students sometimes approach such questions with a casual attitude and instead of taking the question as an opportunity to demonstrate their knowledge they provide extremely brief and uninformative answers.

For example, in part (a) of the question a good answer would demonstrate a knowledge of different types of companies and should conclude by suggesting a private company limited by shares would be appropriate for Jack and Gill. The good answer would have explained why a limited liability company offers Jack and Gill limited liability and why a public company would be impractical for them at this stage in the development of their business. You may even be able to explain why they could not trade as a guarantee company.

In part (b) you would need to discuss how many members are needed to set up a limited company. The good student may take the opportunity to demonstrate further knowledge by explaining that you can set up a private single member company.

Part (c) would require you to show knowledge of the legal requirements when appointing directors and secretaries. In this case if Jack was to be the only director he could not be the company secretary too. A good student may wish to show that common sense suggests that being the managing director and company secretary, even if there was another director, would not be a good idea as the demands made upon the person trying to fulfil both these roles would be difficult to perform.

Part (d) really follows on from (c) and demonstrates that a person can be a secretary and director of a company provided they are not the only director.

Part (e) gives you the opportunity to show that you understand the rules relating to the purchase of shares in public and private companies. The basic answer would probably only say that they cannot offer their shares for sale in the newspaper. The better answer would explain that private companies cannot offer their shares for sale to the public and advertising in a newspaper would be such an offer. Only public companies can do this. Private companies must sell their shares by private treaty.

10. See Chapter 7, Section 1.

This is essentially an essay-type question which should give the good student an opportunity to demonstrate his knowledge of this area of employment law. The answer could be supported by several useful case examples which would show an awareness of its application.

The question asks two interrelated questions. A student who merely states the tests for distinguishing an independent contractor from an employee will gain adequate marks but a student who can support the tests by case examples will earn better marks. Sometimes students attempt to answer questions of this nature without really understanding the question. You must be able to explain what the difference is between a contract of service and a contract for services to attempt this question. Using everyday examples to illustrate your answer would demonstrate your understanding. For example, showing that 'employing' someone to come and fit a new central heating system in your house is a contract for services, making the person an independent contractor whereas someone who is employed everyday as a shop assistant in a department store is likely to be an employee of the department store.

The second part of the question asks you to explain why it is important to distinguish between the two for employment purposes. This requires you to discuss matters such as employment law rights, which are not available to independent contractors and the vicarious liability of employers for their employees.

INDEX